POLITICS, SYMBOLS AND POLITICAL THEORY

Rethinking Gandhi

POLITICS, SYMBOLS AND POLITICAL THEORY

Rethinking Gandhi

ASHA KAUSHIK

RAWAT PUBLICATIONS
Jaipur and New Delhi

ISBN 81-7033-651-1

Published by
Prem Rawat for ***Rawat Publications***
Satyam Apts., Sector 3, Jain Temple Road, Jawahar Nagar, Jaipur - 4 (India)
Phone: 0141 651748 / 657006 Fax: 0141 651748
e-mail : rawatbooks@pinkline.net

Delhi Office
G-4, 4832/24, Ansari Road, Daryaganj, New Delhi 110 002
Phone: 011-3263290

Typeset by Rawat Computers, Jaipur
Printed at Nice Printing Press, New Delhi

For
ASHUTOSH

Contents

Contents

Preface

The present work is an enquiry into a largely unexplored area in social sciences, namely, the interaction of politics, symbols and culture, in both theoretical and applied perspectives. Making subtle distinctions between the 'symbolist' and the 'symbolic' and between 'symbols in politics' and 'political symbols', the study seeks to reinterpret Gandhian philosophy and praxis in terms of political symbolism.

The study attempts to bring out how the shift in perspective—from the received western worldview to a 'rooted' point of view—might alter the fundamental categories, methodology and self-understanding of a society in its own setting and relatedness to the outer world and ascertains the salience of Gandhian framework in this paradigm shift. The Gandhian worldview, it is argued, is a 'displacement' of the logic of the modern western paradigm of 'growth-development-modernization' and 'replacement' of the same by an Indian civilizational argument, in favour of a non-hegemonic, liberatory-communitarian order.

It is further argued that in his long, sustained struggle for liberating India from politico-economic oppression and socio-cultural subjugation, Gandhi questioned not only the 'how' of the 'liberal-industrial-capitalist' combine but also the 'why' of their superimpositions on the non-west. Also, in order to reclaim the 'present' Gandhi thought it imperative to reclaim the past, not in a wholesale manner, but as selective-adaptation of its meaningful heritage. This was a specific mode of engagement with culture. It is important to note that far from being an alibi for *status quo*, Gandhi's engagement with culture ---through a consciously devised symbolism---was a singular stance of radical vision and innovative political praxis. To address the Gandhian alternative is, thus, to address and confront the challenging ethos of our times in relation to both our heritage and the current options at our disposal.

The presentation is simultaneously a historical analysis and a trans-historical extrapolation of Gandhian ideas in contemporary context. The former aims at ascertaining Gandhi's own meaning in his own times and the latter his significance today. At first glance, the study might appear a supererogatory exercise, excavating what is quite above the ground. It is hoped that such a judgement will be disconfirmed by the ensuing analysis.

The study was begun initially as a post-doctoral project. My grateful thanks are due to the ICSSR for awarding me Senior Fellowship to work on the project. I also take this opportunity to express my veneration and gratitude to my teachers---late Prof. Iqbal Narain and Prof. D.B. Mathur---for the valuable guidance, I always got from them.

It is a pleasant duty to acknowledge with thanks the cooperation extended by the library staff of various libraries: Gujarat Vidyapeeth and Sabarmati Ashram, Ahmedabad; American Studies Research Centre (now IACIS), Hyderabad; Nehru Memorial Museum and Library, Delhi; Vinoba Gyan Mandir and Kumarappa Sansthan, Jaipur; Centre for Gandhian Studies and Central Library, University of Rajasthan, Jaipur.

The work might not have acquired the present form but for

the cheerful forbearance of Dr. Surendra, Ashlesha and Ashutosh. The study owes to them much more than words can express.

Finally, I am thankful to Rawat Publications for expeditious publication of the book.

Asha Kaushik

1

Symbols and Politics

A Theoretical Formulation

"Men possess thoughts, symbols possess men."[1]

A symbol is a complex of ideas, images, meanings and experiences, rooted in a social milieu and a cultural tradition and yet possessing a trans-contextual character. It is at once an epistemological signification to comprehend the cognitional and existential universe as well as an objectification of experience, expressing both a living intercourse among people and an accumulated knowledge of the past. At the theoretical level, moving beyond the long-known epistemological sensory-rational problematic, traceable to the ancient Greek distinction of *neumenon* and *phainomenon*, resulting advertently or inadvertently in a sort of mutation of consciousness, symbols point towards the horizon of 'composite consciousness'. As objectification of experience, symbols represent and explain the *deiknymenon* (the seen), *legomenon* (the said) and *dromenon* (done) as ever-changing, in both esoteric and exoteric terms.

In political terms, symbols though rooted in a cultural context, are not mere cultural consequences. Often, change is perceptible in their meaning as "political instrument" and as normative archetypal representation of analogous cognitional and existential reality, that is signified and is active in shaping politics. Assuming that the subject activity of man has an objective content, the accumulated knowledge of the past, its heritage and norms are transmitted from one generation to another in the form of culture. In the given socio-cultural universe then, symbols as expressive and communicative practices acquire the status of action with the potential of facilitating political praxis. Thus interpreted, symbols in politics are valuable as both 'cultural idiom of politics' and political ideals and practices.

Generally speaking, a symbol stands for, represents or denotes something else, beyond the given object or idea. Etymologically, 'symbol' is traceable to the Greek word *symbolon*, meaning contract, token, insignia and a means of identification. Parties to a contract, allies, guests and their host could identify each other with the help of the parts of the *symbolon* in ancient Greece. In its original meaning, the symbol represented and communicated a coherent greater whole by means of a part. The part, as a sort of certificate, guaranteed the presence of the whole and, as a concise meaningful formula, indicated the larger context. The symbol, in this sense, was based on the principles of representation, complementarity and mutual recognition.

The symbol-objects such as the picture, the sign, the word or the gesture require the association of certain concrete ideas in order to fully express what is meant by them. To this extent, it has an esoteric and at the same time, an exoteric, or a veiling and a revealing function. The discovery of its meaning presupposes a certain amount of active cooperation between the symbol-user and his audience. As a rule, it is based on the convention of a group that agrees upon its meaning. Symbols, however, may also be individually and subjectively constructed.[2]

It is notable that historically speaking symbols were used in religious practices to convey ideas concerning man's relationship with the sacred and the spiritual. Non-religious symbols on the other hand having achieved increasing significance in the nineteenth and twentieth centuries, deal with man's relationship to, and conceptualization of, the material world. Rational, scientific-technical symbols have assumed an ever-increasing importance in modern science and technology. Such non-religious secularized symbols also function in a manner similar to religious symbols by associating a particular meaning with a particular sign. Rationalization of symbols, symbolic complexes, and myths have been in evidence, at least, since the Renaissance.[3]

Allegories, personifications, figures, analogies, metaphors, parables, pictorial representation of ideas, signs, emblems as individually conceived symbols with added verbal meaning and attributes used for distinguishing certain persons, are formal, historical and literary categories of the symbolical. If one looks for a definable common denominator for the various types of symbols, one could perhaps choose the term 'meaning sign' to best describe the simultaneous revealing and the concealing aspects of experience. The symbol involves the acknowledgement (from those to whom it is communicated) of the experience that it expresses. Sometimes it goes beyond the obvious meaning for those who contemplate its depths. It indicates the need for communication and yet conceals the details and the innermost aspects of its contents.[4]

The function of the symbol is to represent reality or truth and to reveal them either instantaneously or gradually. As Goethe has note, "in true symbolism, the particular represents the universal, not as a dream or shadow, but as a living revelation of the unfathomable". The relationship of a symbol to reality is at times identified with the reality that it represents and is often regarded as a pure transparency. The representation of the experience, and relationship to reality has either a denotative or a truly representative meaning. A symbol in its intermediary function comprises aspects of epistemology and ontology. As a means of knowledge, it operates in a characteristically dialectical process of veiling and revealing truth. Mircea Eliade has argued that the symbol reveals certain aspects of reality, the deeper aspects, which defy any other means of knowledge.[5] And, even if it is accepted that the claims of the symbolists, of approaching truth/reality through symbols in a unique way, are untenable largely, symbols undoubtedly fulfil an interpretative function in the process of effectively apprehending and comprehending experience. In doing so, the symbol with its meaning, contextual use, relationship with other types of expression and interpretative connection with the various forms of sign, picture, gesture and sound, plays an important part in the process of symbolical perception and reflection. The symbol functions in these ways because it has an analogous cognitional as well as existential relationship to that which it signifies.

Symbols originate in sense impressions or in objects of environment. Some of them are derived from the objects of nature and others are artificially constructed in a process of intuitive perception, emotional experience or rational reflection. In most cases, the constructions are again related to objects in the world of sense perception. A tendency toward simplification, abbreviation into signs and abstraction from sense objects is quite evident, as also the tendency to concentrate several processes into a single symbol. The meaning of individual symbols may change in both positive and perverted senses.

The foundations of the symbolization process lie in the spheres of the conscious and the unconscious, of experience and thought, of sense perception, intuition and imagination. Sensation, physiological and psychological processes also play an important role in the formation of the symbol structure as do the processes of rational conceptualization and structuralization. Thus, there is marked correlation between sense perception, imagination and the work of intellect.[6]

The symbol has a long established relationship with myth (entrenched over time, sacred and esoteric), often manifesting a collection of symbolic forms, actions, expressions and objects. Myths depict gods, demons, men, animals, plants and material objects, as bearers of symbolical meanings and intents. Sometimes it is difficult to distinguish between a myth and a coherent complex of symbols brought together as parables. Some notable examples are myths of cosmogony (origin of the world), theogony (origin of the gods) and anthropogony (origin of man). Religious teaching, dogma and theology also formulate symbolic values or refer to traditional symbolic representations.[7]

The field of symbolism and iconography shows a strong interdependence that existed between religion and other areas of culture, later to become autonomous and profane or secularistic. The social domain develops its own symbolism for expressing values and objectives. Conversely, religion often draws its symbols from social, political and economic domains. Some of the instances of such motifs could be cited as throne, crown, spectre, standard arms, instruments, the figures of father, mother, child, and symbols of familial relationships. The morals, laws, administration of justice, customs and habits of a society inhere in religious symbols and symbolical actions such as anointing a king and administering of oath, trial by ordeal or observance of traditions and customs associated with birth, marriage and death.[8]

Symbols have also achieved new significance in the conceptual presentations of distinctly scientific systems, for instance, in physics, cosmology, psychiatry and psychology.

Although symbols tend to be normative and stable and also have a fixed meaning value, the demise of old symbols and emergence of new ones, or changes in the meaning of existing symbols, nevertheless, occur frequently. The disintegration of individual symbols and change in emphasis on the role of symbolism in general are partly consequences of cultural, intellectual, social and economic transformations.

In the long history of the forms of symbolical expression, a narrower (exclusive) and a broader (inclusive) idea of "what a symbol is", has gradually evolved. This is reflected in the various manners of symbolical expression that influence and combine with one another. Just as the ideology and terminology of the ancient Greek mystery (salvatory) religions distinguished between what was shown and seen (*deiknymenon*), what was done (*dromenon*) and, what was said (*legomenon*), so also symbols could be distinguished as 'the visual', 'the linguistic', and 'the action-oriented'.[9]

Symbolic aspects were de-emphasized by Eighteenth Century Rationalism. However, during the age of Romanticism (around 1760-1870), the importance of 'the symbolical' for religion was rediscovered and revived, more significantly in the works of the English poet and artist, William Blake and theologian, Friedrich Schleirmacher, the philologist and archaeologist, George Friedrich and the Roman Catholic author, Joseph Von Gorres.[10] Symbolist aesthetics originated in the anti-realist movement of the late nineteenth and early twentieth centuries, in French literature, especially poetry, and spread to painting and theatre, influencing the arts in varying degrees elsewhere in Europe and in America, as a reaction against Parnassian Poetry, the Realist Theatre and the Naturalist Novel, seeking to express symbolically, the underlying mystery of existence.[11]

Subsequently, symbols did not remain confined to theology or to aesthetics but constituted valuable means of insight into cognitive and depth psychology, anthropology, social psychology, linguistics and philosophy, with possible new dimensions for political analysis and political epistemology, especially bearing upon studies of political learning, education, socialization and most significantly, communication.

Anthropological studies demonstrate that the major difference between man and other living creatures is the former's use of signs as symbols. Thus interpreted, with the evolution of symbolism and the symbolic processes, came the growth of human civilization. It was the exercise of the symbolic faculty that brought culture into existence and it is the use of symbols that makes the perpetuation of culture possible. In the absence of 'the symbolic' it is argued that there would be no culture and man would be merely an animal, only a sub-human.[12]

The central assumption of all subsequent social theorizing has been that all living creatures adjust and readjust, respond and react, to the environment that operates *within* and *around* them. Some pursue this more intensively and skilfully than others. The pursuit, in general, is understood as learning-adaptation-understanding, at various levels of perception and cognition through various skills and channels of communication, inclusive of the 'symbolic.'

It is Ernst Cassirer who is credited with the pioneering philosophico-cultural enunciation of, what could be termed as, symbology. He has argued that symbolic representation is an essential function of the human consciousness and is basic to our understanding of language, history, science, art, myth and religion. In his view, symbolic forms have been instrumental in the advancement of humans to their present eminence in the world. Charles Peirce elaborated upon symbolic logic with reference to convention, habit or agreement.[13]

For Carl Jung, symbols are 'natural'—prior to their cultural manifestation—because they reach down to and express the unconscious in primitive fashion at the same time as they correspond to the highest intuitions of consciousness. Also, the symbols of the self in Jung's view arise in the depths of the body and they express its materiality every bit as much as the structure of the perceiving consciousness.[14]

In the confrontation between 'natural' and 'conventional', 'individual' and 'social' as criterion in the definition of symbols, questions have arisen, Raymond Firth rightly argues, as to how far differences in consciousness or intention are relevant to the process of representation.[15] Opinion has varied on this issue. Susan Stebbing and S.F. Nadel are preferentially concerned with conscious, even designed representation.[16]

Psychologists point out that individuals select, organize and interpret sensory stimulation into a meaningful and coherent picture of the world, through what is generally known as perception.[17] Although perception is the way things look to us or the way they sound, feel, taste, or smell, it also involves to some degree, an understanding, awareness, recognition or meaning for the perceiver.[18] Perception is not only closely related to the learning process, it also involves a conception of one's own self-image, needs, values and purposes, as much if not more than it involves the image of the object perceived. Symbols are a determining constituent in this entire process.

Psychoanalysts have also shown how closely intertwined and well-integrated are the private and the public symbols of men. Cognition is important in this process. Cognition is generally related with the organization of representational structures of perception of both internal and external phenomena. As the individual's cognitive structure grows, so does his ego and goal images as well as values, attitudes and expectations associated with each of them.[19] Perception and cognition are complements of the learning process, a result of experience, a given stimulus (input) eliciting a different response (output) than it did before.[20] A critical aspect of learning is the adaptation process. Cognitions become mutually dissonant if the obverse of one follows from the other. Cognitive dissonance refers to a relation among cognitions, knowledge, opinions or beliefs which exist simultaneously for a person.[21] A political activist's principal skill faces the challenge of management of language and symbols so as to reduce cognitive dissonance.

At the social level, individuals cannot exist outside communication, which is primarily a means of uniting individuals and is conducive to their development. This explains the simultaneous existence of communication as both the necessity and the reality of social and interpersonal relations.[22] Relevantly interpersonal relations, as distinguished from the general structures of social relations, have an emotional basis. For instance, 'conjunctive' emotions bring people closer together, whereas 'disjunctive' emotions disconnect and divide, though in actual practice human relations are not confined to direct emotional contact but are also mediated by joint activities.[23]

Symbols serve as stores of meaning in communication. Performance of a symbolic act allows ideas to be shared and reformulated without use of words or with minimal verbalization. The meanings of the symbols are, thus, socially produced, even if personally interpreted. The meanings of the symbols are inculcated by social processes of learning. Symbols as stores of meaning thus help to cope with problems of communication over time.

The peculiarities of human communication, therefore, do not allow it to be considered only in terms of the theory of information. However, the concept of the 'purposefulness' of signals employed therein, is a useful tool for explaining the 'exial' (when signals are directed towards individual people) and the 'retial' (when signals are directed towards a larger number of addressees) communication process. In both cases, however, a social orientation is facilitated, since the dispatching of the signals to the group forces the recipients to identify with a sense of belonging.[24]

Increasing importance of the interactive aspects of communication led to the formation of a special direction in social psychology, considering interactions as the starting point of every socio-psychological analysis, known as 'symbolic interactionism'. Following William James, Herbert Mead explained the social nature of the human 'self' stating that interaction played a decisive role in the formation of this 'self'.

Interactions in Mead's framework, are determined by a system of symbols, meaning activities and behaviour of the individual in situations of interactions, which, in the final analysis, depend on the symbolic interpretation of these situations. Although Mead's theory is called the theory of 'symbolic interactionism', it does not, in essence, distinguish between the two different aspects in communication: as an exchange of information, and as organization of joint activities.[25]

While language as a tool of information-transmission commands upper-most attention among students of human communication, the non-linguistic sign-processes have also assumed significance. Psychologists have, in the recent past, developed a science of gestural communication, known as *Kinesics*, devoted to analyzing paralinguistic phenomena on the assumption that it is possible to code body motions such as facial expressions, gestures and postures in ways analogous to the coding of written and spoken language. Imaginative politicians may adopt a personal gesture as a kind of trademark.

Pictorial signs abound in the political art of election campaign posters, political emblems, portraits of national heroes and variety of political propaganda. Non-linguistic sounds carrying political information may be heard in national anthems, campaign music, the distinctive gesture of a political leader or the roar of gun fire. However, information transmitted by non-linguistic signs runs the particular risk of producing ambiguous messages or errors of encoding. Symbols can be convenient objects of devotion or defiance. They may express the hegemonic values of the ruling classes, or the democratic/protestant ethic of those who defy the established order. Symbols can be rallying points for collective action in a specific direction. They can also be used for justifying social stasis.

A physical thing may be a *sign* in one context and a *symbol* in another. This has caused some confusion in establishing the differences between sign and symbol. In a sign-context, the meaning of a word can be grasped with the senses. In a symbol-context, the meaning of a word cannot be perceived with the senses but is created and bestowed arbitrarily by the observer. Conventional symbolism is simply the acceptance of an initial user's meaning or value of the symbol by subsequent users.

Certainly, a symbol may have the form of a material object, a colour, a sound, an odour, a motion, a taste. The meaning or value of the symbol, however, is in no instance derived from or determined by properties intrinsic to its physical form. For instance, the cloth and colour of a flag have little intrinsic meaning, but they attain exceptional significance when used as a symbol to represent a nation. Susanne Langer has argued that symbols differ from signs by their greater articulation and presentation of 'concepts'. A sign, in her view, is comprehended if it serves to make us notice the object or situation, it bespeaks a symbol if it makes us conceive the idea it presents.[26] According to Charles Morris, a symbol is a sign that is produced by its interpreter and that acts as a substitute for some other sign of which it is synonymous.[27] Peirce and Stebbing also consider the position of the interpreter significant in deciphering the meaning of a symbol.

John S. Nelson points out that "literalists of all kinds, behaviourists included, are inclined to confuse symbols with signs, which make one to one mappings". Studies of political beliefs and learning have tried repeatedly to reduce symbols to signs, either overtly through operationalizations intended to divide symbols into many discrete dimensions or scales of meaning, or covertly through technical usage of terms to the same effect. Less programmatically, similar attempts occur through determined misinterpretation or sheer avoidance of phenomena, dense in symbols. For sometime, researchers have been seeking substantive theories which explore learning as a symbolical activity. There is little in politics that is not significantly symbolical and in Nelson's view, a strategic advantage of studies in political socialization is their lead in illuminating this aspect for political enquiry.[28]

The symbolical realities are too intricate and fluid for the analytically fixed concepts of literalist inquiry to comprehend and explain. True, sign-oriented methods are significant in terms of epistemologies of stimulus and response theories, taken most seriously by the behaviouralists. Like the closely related epistemologies of logical positivism and empiricism, these rely on simple correspondence theories of truth, which seek one-to-one correlations between words and atomistic bits of the physical world. Similarly, related theories of psychology readily devolve into various meta- and pseudo-theories, more as groundless rules for language rather than as substantive conceptions of reality. This should wean students of political socialization away from behaviourism in psychology as much as behaviouralism in political science.[29] Serious concern for symbols departs from sign-based epistemologies and theories alike. It leads towards symbolic epistemologies such as those projected by some cognitive and depth psychology theories.[30]

The tension between taking symbols seriously and retaining objectivism is nowhere more evident than in the depth psychology of Sigmund Freud, who strained long and unsuccessfully to reconcile objectivist terminology and epistemology with symbolical psychology.[31] Studying structures and dynamics of desire through the lens of symbol, Freud and others have reopened epistemology to the realms of will, appetite, emotion and imagination. No longer limited to narrow notions of reason, promoted by the modernity paradigm (especially, the Enlightenment), epistemology can comprehend not only what we *see* but also what we *want*.[32] This only underlines the necessity to take into account the intricate interplay of knowledge and desire.

Positivist attempts at substantiating the reliability of scientific knowledge through rejection of the sense-perception and banishing philosophical questions as 'metaphysical', lying outside the sphere of science, have not been successful. In fact, the roots of the objectivist dichotomy of emotion and reason lie in the long-known epistemological sensory-rational problematic, resting on the ancient Greek distinction between the mentally comprehended (*noumenon*) and what is comprehended by the senses (*phainomenon*). This kind of rupture between 'sensibility' and 'rationality' has resulted in an antinomy of conceptions and what may be described as more dangerous, a sort of 'mutation of consciousness'. Symbols may be utilized in regaining the composite character of consciousness, comprising both reason and emotion.

Several notable theoretical attempts have been made in the direction of resolving the aforesaid dichotomies, such as the probability theories,[33] objective and rationalist idealism,[34] intuitionism,[35] natural materialism,[36] pragmatism[37] and methodological anarchism.[38] One might concede the profundity of the claim that if conceptual thought cannot be directly deduced from sense experience, a more viable identification of link must be sought that would explain the transition from the sensory to the rational.[39]

Several cognitive and depth psychological theories also avoid dichotomies of reason and emotion and caution against reifying such mental 'structures.' Analyses of reason as emotion checking emotion, desire righting desire, or feeling balancing feeling, and rationality being pluralized as 'styles' or complexes of cognition-cum-emotion are significant in this context.[40] Cognitive and depth psychological theories throw useful light on conceptions of choice, even though action is not their central concern. Symbolistically understood, reason is compatible with freedom and choice, since such flexible connections allow recommending alternatives and options in terms of 'the rational' as the imaginative, emotive and even appetitive. Symbols, thus, emerge as interactive complexes of reason, imagination and emotion. They are at once cognitive and affective.

Taken as elements of the cognitive activity, symbols are shorthand expressions for a complex of ideas, images and experiences extending into a rich range of associations. Sometimes, the 'symbolic' is understood as equivalent to 'notional' or 'fictional'. It is suggested that whatever be the feelings generated by the 'symbol', the appropriate action would not be forthcoming, implying a manifest separability of feeling and action and even a contrast of 'symbol' with 'reality'. It is little realized in such interpretations that 'symbolic/symbolist thinking' reveals the deeper aspects of reality, the hidden modalities of life. The supposition that symbols refer only to the spiritual (and non-material) realm, is rather ill-founded. Mircea Eliade, in one of the most illuminating expositions of symbolic thought, explains the interconnection between humans and the cosmos, society and nature, through what he calls 'hierophanies'—manifestations of the sacred in the secular world, represented by symbols. In his view, "symbols identify, assimilate and unify diverse levels and realities that are to all appearance incompatible."[41]

Several sociological theories have also offered substantive accounts of socialization, acculturation and education and rich conceptions of symbolism. Notable among them are:

symbolic interactionism,[42] neo-Marxism,[43] phenomenological interpretations,[44] structuralism[45] and cultural evolutionism.[46] Ideology has been a central concern of these theories. Ideology as a conception of knowledge rests on an interrelated comprehension of emotion, evaluation, politics, rhetorics, as part of the concern for an interactive continuum of politics, culture and symbols, traceable in varying degrees to Freud, Marx and Manheim. As discussed earlier, the interactive ideological conception attends to the categories of political learning and the media of political communication. In turn, issues of political communication should lead to an emphasis on the actual contours of political interaction, which is also related to the various practices that constitute the political world. Relating to practices is also a mode of overcoming the objectivist doctrine that categories from everyday discourse are necessarily suspect and inferior to academic discourse.

If it is true that human history is possible because there are concrete living people, it is equally true that the 'subject activity' of man has an 'objective' content, just as his subjective experience has. Experience, in a broad sense, denotes man's attitude to the external world as that of a subject capable of practical activity and possessing consciousness. Since human activity has a mediated character, this character must be carried into human experience. The unity of the sensuous and the rational aspects of human activity thus functions as a unity of its practical and cognitive dimensions. Human experience is objectified in concrete form, in terms of 'humanized nature', and also expressed in terms of language, symbols and signs. Symbols, thus interpreted, are the 'objectification of experience,' signifying both the living intercourse of people and the accumulated knowledge of past experience and contribute to the creation of 'composite consciousness' or what Raymond Williams calls 'practical consciousness' in society.[47]

Drawing on ideas, images and experiences, a symbol far

from being unidimensional, is inherently synthesizing through connections and comparison, never through reduction.[48] These suggestive, flexible connections of symbols account for the crucial processes of not only learning and socialization, but also communication and mobilization.

What Philip Wheel Wright has written of the 'tensive symbol' holds true for any actual symbol as it "cannot be entirely stipulative, in as much as its essential tension draws life from a multiplicity of associations, subtly and for the most part subconsciously interrelated, with which the symbol, or something like it and suggested by it, has been joined in the past, so that there is stored up potential of semantic energy and significance, which the symbol, when adroitly used can tap."[49]

True, symbols in essence are 'representational', but their potential is not exhausted by merely communicating the desired message of 'truth' conceived and interpreted as reality but significantly extends to a "shared construction of reality".[50] In fact, as symbolic thinking precedes language and discursive reason, it reveals the deeper aspects of reality. It is for this reason that reality is often indistinguishable from its symbolization and is better understood in terms of the entire range of associations that are invoked in the process. When Max Lerner observes that "men possess thoughts but symbols possess men", he reminds us of the enormous power that symbols possess in meaningfully relating the abstract to the concrete, the general to the particular, and one may add, the cultural to the political. Symbols and their context far from being static, are always in motion and hence in need of reinterpretation, re-adaptation and sometimes, even of 'inversion'.

In politics, symbolism operates at multiple levels in multiple forms. It is not for the abstract, incomprehensible, metaphysical attributes that symbols are valuable in politics but for their comprehending, communicative, mobilizing and praxiological potential. The key to an understanding of their symbolic quality, as rightly stressed by Raymond Firth, is in the circumstances to which they refer or of which they are a part.[51] It is not their particular nature but the range of relationships that account for their selection as symbols. This process, it is important to remember, involves a constant interpretation and reinterpretation of both symbols and their context—social, cultural, political. Symbols, if not re-adapted and reinterpreted, lose their meaning, appeal and power and become redundant. This is more true in the political realm than elsewhere.

Living, vibrant, contextual symbols "furnish the means by which people make sense of the political process."[52] Michael Novak thinks of politics as "primarily the art of understanding the symbols actually operative in society and learning how to make them issue forth in action."[53] The symbolic, in this sense, is not a residual dimension of politics, and in Kessler's view, "still less an insubstantial screen upon which real issues are cast in pale and passive form". The symbolic, in a particular sense, is real politics articulated in a special and often the most powerful way.[54] It is, therefore, necessary, as Geertz argued long back, "to understand how the symbolic enters into politics, how political actors consciously or unconsciously manipulate symbols and how this symbolic dimension relates to the material bases of political power."[55] As, it is through symbols that people give meaning to their lives to a large extent, "full understanding of political allegiances and political action hinges on this fact."[56] For, in essence, people are as much symbol producers as symbol users/manipulators, not only in the cultural/social realm but also the political sphere.

Before we proceed to analyze symbols as 'cultural idiom of politics' in the following pages, it is important to underline that a distinction between 'political symbols' and 'symbols in politics' may be analytically useful in understanding the interface of politics and symbols. 'Political symbols', generally speaking, are specific, expressive and definitive, whereas 'symbols in politics' would indicate a more comprehensive, flexible, complex, inclusive and less definitive interactive process.

In conceptualization of 'political symbols', the contribution of Harold Lasswell and Abraham Kaplan has been most signal in modern political analysis. Defining political symbols as "the perspectives and the instrumentalities of power", they make subtle analytical distinctions between myth, ideology and utopia and between political doctrine, political formula and key symbols. Power itself is classified as formal and effective into authority and control, according to the role of symbols (perspectives) with which it is associated.[57] Political symbols, for them, are symbols that function to a significant extent in power practices.

Political symbols, as stated by Lasswell and Kaplan, "function directly in the power processes, serving to set up, alter, or maintain power practices". Most familiar are the authoritative or semi-authoritative types of political symbols, for instance constitutions, charters, laws, treaties and so on. But there are many other sorts as well. Important among these are party platforms, polemics, slogans, speeches, editorials, forums on controversial subjects, political theories and philosophies. Charles Merriam calls attention to some other forms of political symbolism such as memorial days and periods, public places and monumental apparatus, music and songs, artistic designs in flags, decorations, statuary, uniforms, story and history, ceremonials of an elaborate nature, mass demonstrations with parades, oratory, music.[58]

The connection of political symbols with power practices is not necessarily in terms of what C.W. Morris calls the 'designative' meaning of the symbols. The political significance of the symbol, Lasswell and Kaplan rightly emphasize, may be in its 'appraisive' or 'prescriptive' meaning. The bearings of the symbol on power relationships may result from the feelings it arouses or action it incites rather than from the objects or states of affairs symbolized. The analysis of political symbols often requires a distinction between manifest and latent content of symbols. The manifest content—the literal, direct, or obvious significance—may be far removed from power practices and relations. The symbol may purport to stake a non-social fact or express a non-power demand, but its latent content may be directly political.[59]

Political symbols are global or parochial according to the territorial range of their significance, general or special according to the range of practices signified, universal or particular according to the logical form of their presentation. Lasswell and Kaplan define these concepts as polar/comparative, and explain them in terms of 'expansion' and 'contraction' of symbols.[60] Of particular significance in politics is the "public presentation of political symbols". In fact, that is the crux of political praxis. Lasswell and Kaplan enumerate several variables in this regard: optimism, the ability of the group to withstand deprivation, the perspectives of the potential supporters—the taking up of identifications in the expectation of ensuring indulgence, power position *vis-a-vis* rival claimants for group control, long continued deprivation of the self by the self.[61] Political symbols assume the form of propaganda when manipulated for the control of public opinion and 'ideology' when they deal with matters of consensus. The 'political myth' comprises the "fundamental assumptions" about political affairs. It consists of the symbols invoked not only to explain but also to justify specific power practices. The 'political doctrine' is the part of the political myth that formulates basic expectations and demands. Frequently, political theory serves chiefly to embody political doctrine. Another component is the corpus of various elaborations of social norms, the theories of what is right, good and proper.

Equally significant, probably more significant, are the 'miranda', the symbols of sentiment and identification in the political myth. They are those whose function is to arouse admiration and enthusiasm, setting forth and strengthening faiths and loyalties. They not only arouse emotions indulgent to the social structure, but also heighten awareness of the sharing of these emotions by others, thereby promoting mutual identification and providing a basis for solidarity. Charles Merriam distinguishes 'miranda' (things to be admired) from 'credenda' (things to be believed). The political doctrine, thus, provides the key symbols and unquestioned axioms on which the justification of the social structure rests.[62]

'Ideology' is interpreted by Lasswell and Kaplan as the political myth functioning to preserve the social structure and the 'utopia' to supplant it. The classification, however, as rightly pointed out, cannot be made in abstraction from the concrete situation in which the symbols function. The part of political myth, describing and prescribing in detail the social structure, is called the political formula. Interpretation of the political formula is determined largely by the holders of power in terms of identification, demands and expectations of the powerful. It is important, however, to note that 'power-holders' vary in the weight of control they exercise over political symbols in general and over the formula in particular.[63]

And finally, defining authority as formal power, Lasswell and Kaplan point out that the actual power structure does not necessarily coincide with that described in the political formula. The ascription of authority always involves a reference to persons accepting it as such. Authority, in this sense, is 'subjective'. This subjectivity results from the symbolic status characteristic of the formal as such, and may be ascribed to other formal concepts, for example, law, as well as authority. Naked power, on the other hand, tends to be exercised in situations where current political myths tend to be widely rejected.[64] Thus, Lasswell and Kaplan successfully demonstrate how the "political interactions of various persons and groups" are "manifested in and affected by symbols".

Karl Deutsch proposes to study symbols from the view-point of communication and organization with specific focus on the concept of autonomy. The basis of autonomy, in his view, consists in a particular pattern of treating information. As much of this information is transmitted by means of symbols, autonomy involves certain ways of treating such symbols. If there are strong tendencies toward eventual failure inherent in all autonomous organizations and particularly in governments, such difficulties in governance, according to Deutsch, can be traced to their propensity to prefer self-referent symbols to new information from the outside world.[65]

Glenn Negley, on the other hand, argues that sense and meaning will not be created by the mere juxtaposition of symbols, however precise they may be in a formal sense. The techniques of communication are useful only if the communicator is reasonably clear about what it is he wants to communicate.[66]

Interaction of politics and symbols has also been studied from the view-point of political socialization, learning and education, as discussed earlier, and significantly as "political rhetoric" by Nelson,[67] and in terms of "symbolic leadership" by O.E. Klapp.[68] Political symbols, more often than not, are double-edged. It has been observed that nothing is more potent than political symbols in generating and sustaining voluntary collective behaviour, but nothing is a greater weight upon communication and understanding than the dust of dead idols. Yet, as Charles Frankel rightly reminds us: "It is possible to be so impressed with the power of symbols as to sacrifice intellectual clarity and to be so wary of political symbols, to distrust them in such a wholesale fashion that one sacrifices the most elementary political realism."

True, as elucidated by Frankel, much of the controversy about the nature and use of political symbols in the last analysis is part of the larger conflict between two alternative strategies for social action. The one looks to the concrete alteration of our institutions for the revival of faith and the restoration of morality. It proceeds on the assumption that symbols are most efficacious when what they represent exists and when this existing thing itself produces the emotions which the symbol leads us to expect, or, if it is some ideal which is symbolized, when that ideal is really an animating and controlling element of behaviour, and when it seems worth the cost of its pursuit. The second alternative looks to the manufacture or revival of symbols as the major path by which faith and morality can be restored; and it credits the empirical and critical analysis of symbols with a major responsibility for what it alleges is the present decline in the strength and character of our convictions and behaviour. And most usually, it seems to feel that the turning away from those institutions which have been the traditional repositories of our most sacred symbols has been the major cause of our troubles, and that a renewed faith in these institutions and their symbols is the essential cure.[69] The two strategies, however, need not always be alternative of each other or mutually exclusive. A 'symbolist strategy' may attempt to synthesize both, in whatever measure.

If we address symbols as 'the cultural idiom of politics' as argued earlier in this chapter, it is possible to comprehend several dimensions of interaction of politics and culture in a fresh perspective. Firstly, in a politico-cultural perspective, the issue of the interpenetration of the 'subjective' and the 'objective', the personal and the political, assumes centrality as the public realm is seen as closely intertwined and integrated with the 'private' sphere of the individual. An attempt at the inculcation of the 'personal' into the 'public realm' reveals the various layers of the subjective dimension of politics, as discussed earlier. Symbols furnish politics with the personal, the emotive and the imaginative on the one hand and with the idealistic and even the rationalist on the other. Secondly, the issue of relating to the past acquires significance in political argument. Instead of disowning or denigrating the past, it is accepted as ever-present in both individual and collective lives in the form of culture, tradition, norms, icons and symbols. The cognitive-pragmatic quest through symbols makes a simultaneous foray into the past and an exploration of the present, possible. Thirdly, cultural continuity and socio-political transformation are taken not as antithetical but complimentary processes. In terms of continuity, the past is relevant for the individuals as for nations to "articulate their historical experiences" in order to "respond to what was done and not done, what was thought and not thought, what was felt and not felt in the past, and to make sense of the voices as well as silences of the past. Past is also invoked for seeking identity or images of identity in both culture and historical experience". Such an articulation is valuable aid to meaningful change.

However, historico-political changes and revolutionary consciousness also lead to a questioning, redefinition, even rejection of 'outmoded' aspects of cultural norms, socio-political institutions and practices, inclusive of symbols. Cultural continuity and social transformation, thus, cannot be comprehended in 'exclusive' terms—as one operating in the absence or at the expense of the other---but as an 'interactive' process, mediated by historical forces as well as transformative consciousness.

Fourthly, the conjuncture of the 'political' and the 'cultural' also takes place in the domain of what is designated as the 'symbols of transcendence'. This conjuncture assumes a variety of forms and shapes. Such symbols of transcendence require a double optic for their interpretation in terms of 'contextualized' as well as 'decontextualized' meanings. Drawing on Paul Ricoeur, R.S. Rajan categorizes politics as the realm of 'signification' and culture as the realm of 'symbolization'. He builds a Kantian argument stating that culture cannot be comprehended solely by way of a 'sociology of knowledge' approach but only by way of *trust* in its symbols.

Rajan interprets politics, culture and symbols with reference to psychotherapy. In psychotherapy, at the stage of 'transference neurosis', the individual is made to re-live his earlier trauma, directed against the symbolic figure of the therapist, alluded as the perpetrator. By re-living his own affective past, the patient has the chance of mastering it. It is the transference situation that can turn his suffering into insight and understanding and thereby begin the process of integration. The transference situation is, thus, essentially a struggle with symbols. In the absence of requisite insight and understanding, the 'symbolic wounds' could prove fatal though paradoxically the struggle with the symbols cannot be avoided or bypassed, for, therein also lies the promise of life and truth. The therapist articulates the 'symbolic consciousness' of the patient and thereby releases, in turn, a movement towards life. Considered in its existential significance, the transference situation is the bringing together of the forces of symbol, consciousness and action. Extending the therapeutic logic to the political context, Rajan formulates: "What transference is to psychotherapy, culture is to political praxis."[70]

The 'symbolic', in his view, is the domain of general or universal meanings that transcend the situational meanings. In other words, the 'symbolic' transcends the 'signific'. When symbols transcend their specific context they may be called 'symbols of transcendence'. From this point of view, culture is the domain of symbols of transcendence. 'Symbols of transcendence' are not mere concepts; but also 'exemplars', that is, presentational concretization of general meanings. In a single concrete symbol is presented a whole wealth of insights; the exemplary symbol is fecund and appears inexhaustible by interpretation. Such exemplars or symbols of transcendence are the units of cultural traditions and culture is the structural complex of exemplars "the architectonic of the symbolic".[71]

True, culture is a realm of the 'symbolic' largely, but not wholly, as Rajan assumes. Also, politics as the realm of action feeds upon the realm of meanings but it does not stop there. We, therefore, seek to propose that as the realms of symbols and politics are grounded in the common psychocultural and normative universe, interface between the two, far from being an unnatural/utopian/regressive social phenomenon, is largely inescapable. Therefore, symbols need to be deciphered, construed and transmuted into concrete ideals and ideas, images and practices for meaningful political praxis. New political symbols, with manifest political intent and content are are also created in the process. The average man's world of diffuse and amorphous ideas, identified as 'latent ideology' by Lane, of emotional dispositions, conceptualized as 'structures of feeling' by Williams and theorized as 'sentiment' by Leighton, may be unorganized and inarticulate, yet not inconsequential, in the political realm.[72] It is important to note how political perceptions and attitudes of the people are influenced, shaped and also changed by the cultural force of symbols, when used with a compelling political motif. The impact, at times, is so enormous that it takes the form of an 'emotional wave' and 'revolutionary consciousness' in one or the other direction. The critical edge is attained when people are confronted with pressing vital issues such as the issues of dignified existence, freedom, equality, identity and fundamental human rights.

It is most pertinent to recall that it was Karl Marx who initiated the systematic analysis of culture in relation to power structures. And later on, it was Gramsci, who through his concept of hegemony, developed the most sophisticated analysis of the relationship of the ideological, cultural and the material bases of political power.[73]

Viewed in Gramscian terms, a political order is not a network of static, unchanging structures and institutions, but an "ever-going hegemonic process". Likewise, culture being the normative core of social practices also forms part of the process of hegemony, of domination of one segment of society over another. Thus interpreted, it is an inclusive form of power-relationships in a complex interlocking of political, normative and social forces. Comprehension of the cultural dynamics in a society is a key to comprehending a political order/context in terms of ideals, goals, values practices and norms. It is also a key to the vital process of socio-economic transformation. This implies a necessary recognition of the actuality of domination and subordination in not only politico-economic but also socio-cultural domains.[74] Protest movements led by radical leaders with an innovative political vision strive and also succeed in striking at the very root of the 'hegemonic apparatus' and transforming the prevailing modes of hegemony. Replacing the 'supportive' hegemonic symbols by revolutionary or 'protest symbols' at the level of popular consciousness may be a Herculean challenge for political praxis, but therein lies a whole range of possibilities for innovations in the political realm.

Involvement with culture, in this sense, is an antidote to political 'non-commitment'. Indeed, it carries with it special political obligations to strike at the root of prevailing hegemonic consciousness, expose the paradoxes, and rebel, through responsible criticism and possible action. Creation of socio-cultural consciousness against repression and injustice gets added relevance in the context of colonial/imperialist hegemony. In times when purely cultural solutions may prove utopian and purely political solutions inadequate, 'symbolist strategies', as a specific form of integral politico-cultural experiment' in political praxis, may meet the challenge more efficaciously than other strategies.

Symbols from the heritage arouse intense emotions that can be harnessed for political objectives, in both negative and positive directions. Symbols are double-edged weapons, as mentioned earlier. Political symbols assume a dated character, when narrowly interpreted and confined to parochial political objectives, but transcend the context, when interpreted in terms of long-term ideals of society.

Political symbolism may, thus, be idealistic as well as programmatic, historical as well as futuristic, regressive as well as revolutionary. Symbolist leadership, thus, plays a crucial role in setting the agenda, direction and appropriate strategy for socio-political transformation at any given point of time.

The present study seeks to explore the interactive dimensions of politics, culture and symbols in both theoretical and applied terms. The focus of the study is Gandhi's philosophy and political praxis, interpreted in a symbolist perspective. As Gandhi's philosophy and praxis are inseparably intertwined, it is argued here that his integral symbolism plays a key role in not only redefining and extrapolating religious/ cultural symbols from India's heritage in 'modern political terms' but also 'inverting' the dehumanizing, divisive, alienating, inhibiting symbols and practices ensuing from them. Where Gandhian symbolism is most ingenious and valuable, it is ascertainable in the innovative key political symbols such as *Swaraj*, *Sarvodaya*, *Satyagraha*, *Swadeshi*, Oceanic Circles, along with a big range of explanatory, supplementary and supportive symbols. These symbols were employed with remarkable political insight by Gandhi as a strategy of communication, communion, articulation, mobilization and political struggle. Gandhian symbolism, though most efficacious as a 'symbolist strategy', in the given historical context, is not dated. It is also trans-historical and universalist in its concerns and implications. The true distinctiveness of Gandhian symbolism, it is argued here, lies in the alternative worldview, rooted in Indian civilization, yet identified with the entire mankind. And, it is this distinctiveness that makes Gandhian symbolism compelling and relevant today in terms of both theoretical discourse and political praxis. That is the *raison d'etre* of the present study.

Notes

1. Max Lerner, *Ideas for the Ice Age*, New York, Viking, 1941, p. 235.
2. See "Symbolism and Iconography" in *Encyclopaedia Britannica*, Vol.17, p.900.
3. *Note* 2, p.901.
4. *Note* 2.
5. Mircea Eliade, *Images and Symbols* (Trans. P. Mairet), New York, Sheed & Ward, 1969, p.12.
6. *Note* 2.
7. *Note* 2, p.903.
8. *Note* 2, p.903.
9. *Note* 2, p.904.
10. *Note* 2, p.900.
11. See "Symbolist Movement," *Encyclopaedia Britannica*, Vol.11, pp. 458-459.
12. Leslie A. White, *The Science of Culture*, New York, Farrar, Strauss and Cudahy, 1959, pp.33-34.
13. See Ernst Cassirer, *The Philosophy of Symbolic Forms* (1923) 3 Vols. (Trans. R. Manheim) New Haven, Yale University Press, 1953-7.

    Also see, Charles S. Peirce, *Values in a Universe of Chance, Selected Writings*, (ed., P.P. Weiner) New York, Doubleday, 1958.
14. Carl G. Jung, *Psyche and Symbol* (ed., Violet S.de Laszlo), New York, Doubleday, 1958, pp. 138 & 318-326.

Also see, Mary Douglas, *Natural Symbols*, London, Cresset, 1970.

15. Raymond Firth, *Symbols: Public and Private*, Ithaca, Cornell University Press, 1973, p. 63.
16. Susan L. Stebbing, *A Modern Introduction to Logic*, London, Methuen, 1998, pp. 10 & 111.

    Also see, S.F. Nadel, *Foundations of Social Anthropology*, London, Cohen & West, 1951.
17. Bernard Berelson and Gary A. Steiner, *Human Behaviour: An Inventory of Scientific Findings*, New York, Harcourt, Brace and World, 1964, p.88.
18. Floyed H. Allport, *Theories of Perception and Concept of Structure*, New York, Wiley, 1957, p.14.
19. See Herbert Simon, *Models of Man: Social and Rational*, New York, Wiley, 1957, pp. 198-99.
20. Alfred Kuhn, *The Study of Society*, Homewood, Ill, Dorsey Press, 1963, p.57.
21. See for details, Leon Festinger, *A Theory of Cognitive Dissonance*, Evanston, Ill, Row-Peterson, 1957.
22. A.N. Leontiev, *Problems of the Development of Mind*, Moscow, Progress, 1972, p.357.
23. For details see, G. Andreyeva, *Social Psychology*, Moscow, Progress, 1980, pp.82-94.
24. *Note 23*, pp.103-5.

    Also see, Timotsu Shibutani, *Society and Personality: An Interactionist Approach to Social Psychology*, New York, Prentice Hall, 1961.
25. Some of the seminal works in this field are: Jurgen Ruesch and Weldon Kees, *Non-verbal Communication*, Berkeley, University of California Press, 1956.

    Edward T. Hall, *The Silent Language*, New York, Doubleday, 1959.

    Erving Goffman, *Behaviour in Public Places*, New York, Free Press, 1963.
26. Susanne K. Langer, *Feeling and Form: A Theory of Art*, New York, Scribner, 1953, p.26.
27. See Charles Morris, *Signs, Language and Behaviour*, Chicago, Chicago University Press, 1945.

28. John S. Nelson (ed.), *What Should Political Theory Be Now?* Albany, State University of New York Press, 1983, p.144.
29. *Note 28*, p.445.
30. See Susanne K. Langer, *Philosophy in a New Key*, New York, New American Library, 1942.
31. *Note 28*, 445-46.
32. For critical insight see M. Horkheimer, *Eclipse of Reason*, New York, Seabury, 1947.

    M. Foucault, *The Order of Things*, New York, Random House, 1970.

    Jacques Derrida, *Writing and Difference* (Trans. Alan Blass), Chicago, University of Chicago Press, 1978.
33. See, Rudolf Carnap, *Logical Foundations of Probability*, Chicago, University of Chicago Press, 1950, and Hans Reichenbach, *The Theory of Probability*, Berkeley, University of California Press, 1949.
34. See, Brand Blanshard, *The Nature of Thought*, Vol. I, New York, Macmillan, 1940.
35. See Gustav Bergmann, *The Metaphysics of Logical Positivism*, London, Longman, Green & Co., 1954.
36. See, Bertrand Russell, *Human Knowledge: Its Scope and Limits*, New York, Simon & Schuster, 1948.
37. John Dewey, *Logic: The Theory of Inquiry*, New York, Henry Holt & Co., 1938, p. 119.
38. See Paul K. Feyerabend, *Against Method: Outline of an Anarchistic Theory of Knowledge*, London, New Left Books, 1975.
39. For a critique See, V.G. Panov, *Emotions, Myths and Theories*, Moscow, Progress, 1985, pp. 11-42.
40. See, Willard Gaylin, *Feelings*, New York, Harper and Row, 1979 and A.O. Rorty (ed.) *Explaining Emotions*, Berkeley, University of California Press, 1980.
41. Mircea Eliade, *Patterns in Comparative Religion*, Princeton, Bollingen Series, 1970 p.455.
42. See Peter L. Berger and Thomas Luckmann, *The Social Construction of Reality*, New York, Doubleday, 1966.

43. See specifically, Jurgen Habermas, *Knowledge and Human Interests*, (Trans. J.J. Shapiro), Boston, Beacon, 1971.

44. See Harold Garfinkel, *Studies in Ethno-Methodology*, Englewood Cliffs, NJ, Prentice-Hall, 1967.

45. See Edmund Leach, *Culture and Communication*, Cambridge, Cambridge University Press, 1972.

46. See Clifford Geertz, *The Interpretation of Cultures*, New York, Basic Books, 1973, and

Marshall Sahlins, *Culture and Practical Reason*, Chicago, University of Chicago Press, 1976.

47. Raymond Williams, *Marxism and Literature*, Oxford, Oxford University Press, 1977, pp. 206-212.

48. Victor Turner, "Process, System and Symbol: A New Anthropological Synthesis," *Daedalus*, 106, 3, Summer, 1977, pp.61-80.

Also See, Roger W. Cobb, "The Belief Systems Perspective," *Journal of Politics*, 35,1, February 1973, pp.121-53.

49. Philip Wheel Wright, *Metaphor and Reality*, Bloomington, Indiana University Press, 1962, p. 95.

50. Richard B. Gregg, *Symbolic Inducement and knowing-A study in the foundations of Rhetoric*, Columbia, University of South Carolina Press, 1984, p.133.

51. *Note 15*, p. 18.

52. David I. Kertzer, *Ritual, Politics and Power*, New Haven, Yale University Press, 1988, p.6.

53. Michael Novak, *Choosing Our King: Powerful Symbols in Presidental Politics*, New York, MacMillan, 1974, p. 23.

54. Clwe S. Kessler, *Islam and Politics in a Malay State*, Ithaca, Cornell University Press, 1978, pp. 244-245.

55. See Clifford Geertz, "Religion as a Cultural System" in Michael Banton (ed.) *Anthropological Approaches to the Study of Religion*, London, Tavistock, 1966, pp. 1-46.

56. Victor Turner, *Dramas, Fields and Metaphors* Ithaca, Cornell University Press, 1974, pp. 140-41.

57. See Harold D. Lasswell and Abraham Kaplan, *Power and Society: A Framework for Political Inquiry*, New Haven, Yale University Press, 1950, pp. 103-141.

58. *Note 57*, p.103.
59. *Note 57*, p.104.
60. *Note 57*, pp. 104-105.
61. *Note 57*, pp. 108-109.
62. *Note 57*, pp. 133-140.
63. *Note 57*, pp. 123-130.
64. *Note 57*, pp. 133-140.
65. Karl W. Deutsch, "Self-referent Symbols and Self-referent Communication Patterns: A note on some pessimistic theories of politics" in L. Bryson et al, *Symbols and Values: An Initial Study*, New York, Harper & Brothers, 1954, pp. 619-646.
66. Glenn Negley, "The Failure of Communication in Ethics" in L. Bryson et al, *Note 65*, p. 647.
67. See for details, John S. Nelson's comprehensive essays on "Political Theory as Political Rhetoric" and "Education for Politics: Rethinking Research on Political Socialization" in John S. Nelson (ed.), *What Should Political Theory be Now?*, Albany, State University of New York Press, 1983, pp. 169-240 & 413-478.
68. See for details, Orrin E. Klapp, *Symbolic Leaders: Public Dramas and Public Men*, Aldine, Chicago, 1964.
69. Charles Frankel, "Liberalism and Political Symbols" in L. Bryson et al, *Note 65*, pp. 361-370.
70. R. Sundara Rajan, *Towards a Critique of Cultural Reason*, Delhi, Oxford University Press, 1987, pp. 2-3.
71. *Note 70*, pp. 22-23.
72. For details See, Asha Kaushik, *Politics, Aesthetics and Culture*, New Delhi, Manohar, 1988, pp. 27-43.
73. For details See, Antonio Gramsci, *Selections from the Prison Note Books*, (O. Hoare and G.N. Smith ed. & trans.), London, Lawrence and Wishart, 1971.

    Also See, David Laitin, *Hegemony and Culture*, Chicago, Chicago University Press, 1986.
74. *Note 72*.

2

Gandhian Symbolism

Precepts and Premises

"I want to write many new things, but they must all be written on the Indian slate."

—Gandhi[1]

Contemporary significance of Gandhi lies as much in the universality of his philosophical precepts as in the 'rootedness' of his socio-political premises, the former authenticating his niche among original thinkers of the world and the latter singling him out as an ingenious interpreter of Indian culture and a distinctive innovator of political praxis. The universal and the particular, the historical and the transhistoric, the ethical and the political, the individual and the collective are blended in his thought rather naturally, endowing his vision at once with radicalism and realism.

Evidently, Gandhian discourse, as any other, was primarily a product of the historical context in which it was situated. The context was characterized on the one hand by the pervasive malaise of colonial political oppression, economic expropriation, social stasis, moral degeneration and apocalypse and by resurgent nationalism on the other. Conscious of India's subject status, Gandhi was above all concerned with refashioning the psychological orientations of the people towards political objects as a prelude to effective mass political struggle. In Gandhi's view, changes enforced by British imperialism, had done irreparable harm to the socio-cultural-economic fabric of India. Therefore, the 'political' was not an isolated index of domination by the alien power. It was hegemonic in the true sense. Therefore, it had to be discerned and fought not only at political but simultaneously at socio-economic, cultural and attitudinal levels as well. Accordingly, Gandhi sought a reformulation and a redefinition of politics, relationship of ends and means, criteria for evaluation of personal and public activity and salience of values, beliefs and ethical dispositions in political praxis.

In this endeavour, he highlighted the uniqueness of India's character in terms of both, an alternative worldview and a distinctive form of political praxis. Gandhi realized the fact that psychological and socio-political attitudes of the common masses could be permitted to remain apathetic, static, orthodox and impervious to the oppressive socio-political reality of imperialist domination, only at the cost of the freedom of the country. What was urgently needed was a comprehensive strategy to ignite the dormant urge of the common people for freedom and liberation. Gandhi attempted to do this through a medium that was not alien or distant but familiar and reliable. Symbols rooted in the familiar cultural heritage as well as in popular consciousness were ingeniously perceived by him to be the right medium in the given situation. The symbols, partly resurrected from the tradition and partly devised by Gandhi, therefore, sought to be the pathfinders of socio-political activism and transformation during the freedom struggle and also of the aspired dream of a just socio-econo-political order for the future.

The historico-empirical significance of symbols as 'objectification of experience' was incontrovertibly established by Gandhi by employing the same for transforming an urban-middle class political movement into a mass liberation struggle. Certainly, it was a novel attempt, engaging the cultural idiom of symbols for the objective of political revolution, unprecedented in world political history. The exceptional 'communicative competence' of what might be called, 'the symbolist strategy' was used equally exceptionally and imaginatively by Gandhi to transform both national psyche and political behaviour of the masses. The range of the operational dimensions of the symbols was expansive—employed variantly for educational, informative, value-imperative, orientating, motivational, communicative purposes, and culminating in the objective of political praxis. An exceptionally significant dimension was the removal of prevalent moral alienation and antagonism between duty and happiness and between individual interest and collective well-being, in the socio-political realm. This was, again, a distinctive Gandhian way of protesting the 'present' and visualizing an alternative mode of power-relationships and social dynamics.

In any discussion of symbolism, the past assumes doubtless significance. The past has been valued as an epitome of pragmatic value in several ways. One salient use, in political terms, has been cultivation of the mind, shaping or changing the perceptions and conduct of generations, in the context of political culture. Comprehension of past political events and ideas has often served as a nodal reference point for subsequent understanding. Norman Jacobson identifies past political ideas as 'political education'[2], and Michael Oakeshott values them as expressing and transforming the accumulated political wisdom of a culture.[3] Michael Walzer, commenting on Ludwing Wittgenstein has stressed upon the tradition of "detached judgments by philosophers, even of their own ideologies, practices and institutions."[4] He also talks of the alternative tradition of engagement of sophists, critics, publicists and intellectuals. Elaborating further, Walzer highlights the fact that, Socrates was killed by the 'citizens', "thus demonstrating that engagement and fellowship are not possible for everyone committed to the search for truth."[5] History seemed to repeat itself in the case of Gandhi, instructing again for a ceaseless struggle against injustice.[6]

Significantly, as Nehru, with profound insight, notes: "The whole conception of history in ancient India was influenced by the speculative and ethical trends of philosophy and religion. Facts and fiction are so interwoven together as to be inseparable, and this amalgam becomes an imagined history, which may not tell us exactly what happened but does tell us something that is equally important---what people believed had taken place, what they thought their heroic ancestors were capable of, and what ideals inspired them. So whether fact or fiction, it became a living element in their lives..."[7]

Gandhi realized the tremendous impact this 'imagined history', in the form of mythology and tradition, had on the minds of the people, especially, the uneducated masses in India. He imaginatively made it the basis of political praxis and also future history. This might be taken as a form of cultivated insistence on confronting the past partly in its actual detail and partly through symbols, exemplifying aspects of the vibrant heritage. Admittedly the question of linking the 'historical' with the cognitive,' 'ideational' or the 'theoretical' past is not without controversy.

Gandhi's foray into India's past, therefore, was neither indulgence in nostalgic revivalism, obscurantism, chauvinism nor an escape-route to a primitive utopia, as often alleged. On the contrary, it was a conscious search for rootedness, a part of the critical 'self-searching' and 'self-interrogation,' at the individual as well as the national levels. In Gandhi's view, India's past incorporated a well-ordered and well-developed socio-politico-economic order. More important, he insisted, the ideational and normative core of ancient Indian civilization, extrapolated in contemporary terms, could also be explored as a possible alternative, in contemporary context. Past, in this sense, was a testing ground for the present in terms of critical comparability.

Viewed thus, Gandhian symbolism was an incisive mode of rediscovering India's cultural heritage and also her lost identity. It was a conscious strategy to reawaken pride in one's own self, culture, tradition and nation---not for constricted revivalism or chauvinism---but to look, with confidence and dignity, in the face of the arrogant imperialist west and, more important, to reconstruct Indian society and politics on solid foundations.

The essential greatness of India's spiritual-cultural heritage was epitomized in the Vedantic worldview, systematized and encapsuled in the *Bhagwad Gita*. According to this worldview, the Supreme Reality is the vast undivided whole, *Brahman* or Being, the foundation from which all cosmic manifestation and beings stream forth. The transcendent *Brahman* is present in each particular existence that achieves its true meaning only as it becomes a part of the whole. That which binds it to the *Brahman* is called *dharma*. "Indian Vedantic humanism", as Radhakamal Mukherjee argues, "rooted in the identity of the part with the whole, or the self or *atman* with *Brahman*, is best symbolized and expressed by *dharma*." Mukherjee terms it 'cosmic humanism'.[8]

Metaphysically, *dharma* is *rta* or *chhanda*, denoting the impersonal cosmic order, rhythm or norm. Along with the cosmic dimension, *rta* also has a moral dimension that connotes the social aspects, concretely embodied by *svadha* and *vrata*. The dual-dimensionality of *oughtness* and *goodness* represented by *rta* and *dharma* (as different levels of the cosmic-material, ethico-rational reality) is again superbly synthesized in the *Bhagwad Gita*. It is clearly stated that man is capable of knowing *rta* and realizing it through selfless endeavour, compassion, purity, equanimity and unswerving dedication to the real self, God or *Brahman*. *Dharma*, in this sense, is a fusion of ontology and ethics. It is the law of integral harmony, applying to the cosmic and the social order as well as to the specific course of development of each individual. It is this conception of *dharma* which underlies Gandhian thought and praxis. And, it is of utmost significance to keep this in mind in order to fully understand Gandhian symbolism.

Gandhi's faith in the absoluteness of God led him to state that none of the human formulations of God could be accepted as final. Therefore, equal respect for all systems of faith, organized as 'religions' was essential. It was, in fact, a logical corollary of the diversity of interpretations of the Supreme Being. It was in consonance with this belief, that his prayer-meetings were resonant with hymns from all principal denominational texts. The objective was to inculcate a clearer understanding of one's own denomination as well as of others. It was an exercise in internalizing, to whatever extent, the ideal of *samabhava*, deemed to be most precious by Gandhi in the struggle for *swaraj*. Of equal significance, is the ideal of *lokasamgraha*—redemption of the whole world from ignorance, suffering and evil—which Gandhi draws upon.

Indian spiritual humanism stands for the dynamic progression and universalization of the spirit of every human individual and the illumination and freedom of the entire realm of life—*Jivaloka*. This is the concept of the fusion of the empirical self with the divine self (*Brahman*) and with the social and cosmic order. In concrete terms, it is universal compassion. Gandhi meaningfully adapted this ideal of *sarvamukti*, that is, universal salvation in his architectonic symbolism of *swaraj*. *Sarvodaya*, the ultimate ideal, further epitomised the ethics and politics of love, justice and compassion.

This should also explain the synthesis of dignity and majesty of the individual and universal humanism in Gandhian thought. Moore rightly reminds us that the inert assumption "that cultural and social continuity does not require explanation, obliterates the fact that both have to be recreated anew in each generation often inviting pain and suffering."[9] Gandhi undertook a conscious and concerted 'national mission' to conserve what was worth-conserving in Indian cultural tradition, not as a sentimental urge but as reasoned conviction, faith and pride in its efficacy. Gandhi's plea for resurrection of traditional cultural values through his symbolist strategy, therefore, was not merely an emotive elan but also a 'critical self-searching' as mentioned earlier. He was, indeed, as ruthless in self-criticism at both personal and national levels, as in his indictment of western civilization.

Gandhi was aware that to reconstruct the orientations, attitudes and behaviour of people in a subject-nation, it was first essential to understand their beliefs and values with empathy, and then prepare them for inversion of the oppressive structures and norms, whether imposed by cultural heritage or alien rule.

Gandhi did not hesitate to resurrect symbols from India's tradition and hoary antecedents, but at the same time he was also aware of the stigma of obscurantism, attached to some of them. Accordingly, he reformulated and changed the connotations of such symbols in ample measure with a view to transforming them into efficacious nodal points of revolutionary political praxis and socio-economic transformation.

Religious symbols were very significant in Indian life and Gandhi realized their importance, but at the same time he resisted their absolute acceptance, however long they may have been traditionally observed. Gandhi exposed the superficiality of the esoteric religious rites, as the external expression of religious beliefs and instead, stressed on inner devotion. Stereotyped symbols and practices did not necessarily express human values in his view. He desired to go to the sources on which traditional symbols were based and did not hesitate in questioning or even inverting the cultural codes and hierarchies that subverted human dignity, even though they were supported by scriptural/traditional authority. In fact, as mentioned earlier, when Gandhi talked of Hinduism or of *Sanatana Dharma*, it was more in ontological than in scriptural terms. His interpolation of *dharma* as duty in its broadest manifestation was meaningfully transcribed as *swadharma* and further extended as *samabhava* and *Sarva Dharma Samabhava* in public life, summed up in the key symbol—*ahimsa*.

Gandhi's advocacy of ancient Indian heritage was, thus, strongly qualified by an urge for a higher evaluation of man, discarding discrimination in all forms. If God was 'love' in an ultimate sense, loving all humans as equal beings was a form of devotion (*bhakti*). It was also true deliverance (*mukti*). Logically then, subjection and oppression of one human by another, of one race by another, of one nation by another, is against the laws of God and *dharma*. It is anti-God and anti-*dharma* (*adharma*). Protesting and inverting the same is *dharma* (duty) in a true sense. Hence, Gandhi's symbolism of protest and a material and secular extrapolation of the originally scriptural/religious symbols.

Thus, Gandhian symbolism, though rooted in the ancient Indian tradition, was not circumscribed by it. In fact, Gandhi's signal contribution lay in an undogmatic and unconventional interpretation of Indian tradition and its symbols to suit the needs of a 'modern' national liberation movement. Surfacially, this might sound paradoxical and ironical but in fact, it is not. True, at a more basic philosophical level Gandhi registered not only his protest but absolute rejection of the 'modern' western worldview. He interpreted colonial expansionism as a logical outcome of the 'modern' western industrial-capitalist civilization and ingeniously conceived of Indian civilization as the antidote to the former. It was this counter-hegemonic argument that provided the bedrock for his symbolism. The 'symbolist' was, however, not a residual dimension of politics for Gandhi. It became manifestly political in his hands. He did not superimpose the political meaning on the symbols he was using. The political meaning was imbibed, painstakingly and imaginatively, through a constant process of interpreting and reinterpreting the selected symbols in view of the challenging situation at hand. The guiding spirit, nevertheless, remained unambiguous—a conception of 'what is right' and 'good'. It was Gandhi's way of reconciling "the truth of man with the meaning of history" as V.G. Krishnamurti has succinctly described.[10]

Dispelling the skepticism and apprehension of what Hannah Arendt described as "dark times in which the public realm (was) obscured and people ceased to ask any more of politics",[11] Gandhi resurrected and revived the dignity of a subject-nation and legitimacy of revolutionary political activity, through infusing the public realm with a moral purpose. For in his view the most adverse effect of the imperialist hegemony had been moral degeneration and alienation of Indian masses. Therefore, Gandhi was categorical about the unity of the moral and the political. He repeatedly stated that he could not be leading a religious life unless he identified himself with the whole of mankind and he could not do so unless he took part in politics. Politics, therefore, was taken as a potentially redemptive activity by Gandhi.

He was unambiguous in his appeal to 'principles' (ethical in nature) traceable to the past in India's case, in precedence over adherence to 'rules' (legal formal in nature) glorified in the west. Gandhi did so even at the risk of inevitable conflicts accompanying the broad range of discretion that he bestowed on each individual. This was meant to remind people more emphatically about the 'personal' dimension of responsibility for socio-political action. Interestingly, this was in complete contrast to the concept of 'ordered universe' relentlessly pursued in western political thought, making adherence to rules a precondition for apparent precision in social relations.[12]

Further, neither his 'criticisms' nor his 'remedies' were confined to mere conceptual discourse, as he was extremely sensitive to the possible reduction of conceptual commitment into political constraints. Accordingly, Gandhi's insistence on exemplary ethics and action constituted a distinctive, 'specific' kind of political praxis.

Gandhi thought of moral convictions as intrinsically revolutionary. For him, it is these convictions that endow an individual with courage to make supreme sacrifice for a 'righteous' cause. In the classical Indian tradition, moral-judgment is primarily self-judgment. Gandhi interpreted moral-self-judgment also as moral-obligation (*swadharma*), in consonance with an individual's conscience, or 'inner voice' as he conceptualized it. Fulfilment of moral obligation is not possible without fearlessness (*abhay*). In Gandhi's view, as in Marx's, moral persuasion does not rhyme with notions of physical immortality. Death appears horrible to those who 'individualize' their existence in a morally isolated sense from their social essence. Faith, in the immortality of the self (soul) and of society, is the real source of fearlessness. Assured of his conviction, Gandhi explained to the Indian masses that the freedom movement possessed a profound moral meaning and that without moral regeneration, shaking off of the humiliating imperialist oppression was unthinkable. In addition, Gandhi was also painfully aware of the inner-duality and the inherent disjointedness of the moral subject, of the gap between moral beliefs and unseemly actions. It was a challenging scenario. The colonial situation of oppressive politico-economic relations in India had further widened the above hiatus.

Gandhi, therefore, was faced with the task of demystifying many a cultural code for the common masses. He accomplished it through redefining the abstract principles and conveying the same in the simplest possible form. In the process, Gandhi also explored the everyday source of morality, available in the living folk tradition and even the casual-appearing life-style of the common people. He often insisted on learning from, rather than ostensibly teaching, the common people. It was a unique way of recovering social morality with the power of the symbol. Gandhi endeavoured to bridge the gap between the 'personal' and the 'public' spheres of morality, challenging the prevalent anti-thesis between the 'personally' and the 'socially' valuable. He could, thus, revolutionize the character of politics in India by introducing ethical imperatives in the public realm, and at the same time, endowing those partaking the revolution with a sense of personal responsibility. The latter was particularly significant as the entire revolutionary endeavour was also a simultaneous quest for identity. The quest, as stated earlier, was as much 'individual' as 'national'—'liberation of the whole man' as of the whole nation.

Gandhi's ingenuity lay in generating transformative consciousness without negating cultural continuity. More often than not, he first contextualized and then decontextualized the major religio-cultural symbols, so that they could convincingly carry the political message/content of liberation as he intended. He worked hard for people to realize that the pressing problems of their lives were inseparable from the national problems that the colonial state had created. And, he succeeded, to a large extent, in replacing the 'supportive'/'glorifying' symbols by 'protest' symbols *vis-a-vis* the empire and bringing the ordinary people into the mainstream of the nationalist struggle. What Gandhi attempted was nothing less than a radical redefinition of ends-means relationship.

Thus, symbols in Gandhi's hands did not remain mere legitimizing or explanatory tools, but attained the status of radical political dialectics and praxis. Far from using symbols as pretexts for evading or escaping reality in the name of some obscure ideal of the past, as unjustifiably alleged, Gandhi took symbols as embodiments of reality, and restated their innate meanings and contents. The result was convincing presentation and effective communication. In depth psychology it is described as 'psyche evoking'. This made Gandhian praxis, a specific form of praxis, an effective form, for the power of the invoked symbols was enormous and conversely they invoked enormous power. It was so because the selected symbols were not isolated abstractions but conveyed a whole range of associations---normative and structural. It was probably the most signal fall out of Gandhi's symbolist strategy that people at large could make sense of the colonial situation of oppression and felt obliged to fight the same through Gandhian methods.

Gandhi was convinced that as symbolist actions induced their own likely recurrence in familiar conditions, the same would contribute towards a shared construction of political reality, a unifying common experience, beyond the confines of class, caste, region and religion. When Gandhi ventured to reject the imperial symbols of power, it was an act of stripping them off of glamour, awe and prestige. Thus, challenging the imperial authority people strangely felt a sense of membership in the newly-created political community larger than their own ideas and interests. Gandhi seemed to have awakened them to their lives' mission. It was surely an 'affective' dimension of his symbolist strategy, but also imbued with cognitive, rational political content.

What made Gandhi's appeal effective was his forthright communication with the masses and empathy with their lives, problems and aspirations through decipherable idiom of reciprocal trust. This process informed, articulated and galvanized the masses to identify the forces and causes of their misery and despair under the alien yoke. The symbolist strategy and the genuine humanist concern of Gandhi also substantially bridged the prevailing gap between the political elite and the masses in the freedom struggle.

Gandhi varied, moulded and improvised his interpretation

of the symbols and the style of communication from rational-logical to affective-emotional, according to the target-group he was addressing. His humbling gestures added to his appeal. Even his silences were eloquent. He radiated confidence and trust among people. His self-less demeanour was the strongest asset of his symbolist strategy. His personality personified his ideals and ideas, his message and methods. What is notable, from the point of view of his strategy, is the fact that he did not allow himself to be exploited or mastered by popular symbolism. He remained the master and a master-strategist and skillfully used symbols for both 'psyche evoking' and normative justification of acts of protest.

It is important to note that the real value of a symbol lies in what it is understood as standing for. A master-strategist like Gandhi could grasp how to shape or change the 'understanding' and enhance the power/capabilities of the masses. And, he did so with remarkable balance of mind, avoiding the dangers of both overestimation and powerlessness of the self in the given situation. He stressed firmness with humility and protest with responsibility. He employed symbols as expressible representation of the political message of the revolution and expression of a *radical ethic*, of values of protest. The expressiveness of his symbols was intensified by the imperatives of the historical circumstances.

Gandhi saw symbols as valuable stores of meaning, facilitating communication and sharing of ideas with minimum verbalization and their reformulation, without heavy conceptualization. With rare political insight, he interpreted and reinterpreted the rich corpus of symbols interspersed in the cultural heritage of India---in scriptures, epics, mythologies. As these symbols were well-ingrained in popular consciousness, Gandhi felt confident in employing the same for transformative objectives. He transformed the apparently non-political spiritual ideals into meaningful political motifs and regenerated many a past religio-ethical images in new political forms, with as much vigour as he showed in conceiving new political symbols.

He reinterpreted and reformulated the entire Indian philosophical/metaphysical symbolism of God-truth-virtue in material, socio-political and moral terms. The ideas of God and truth are simultaneously metaphysical and material. Admittedly, God is infinite, and so is truth, unknowable in entirety by human agency. Yet, both God and truth are revealed in the phenomenal world through love, nonviolence. What is significant in Gandhi's reincarnation of God as truth and converse, is that he urges to take the phenomenal world of relative truths seriously. Only a sincere pursuance of the relative truth, as one sees it from time to time, can lead to the realization of the absolute truth. Gandhi perceives *nishkam karma* (selfless action) as enjoined in the *Gita* as the criterion of sincere pursuance. The objective is welfare and service of fellow-beings and of the dispossessed. This is also *dharma* (and *swadharma*). Viewed thus, the ideas of God and truth are also translatable as the idea of 'good'. In fact, the idea of moral good is as universal as truth. In Gandhi, the urge for 'deliverance' is inseparable from the tangible programme of social reconstruction. He has tremendous faith in the innate propensity of man for virtue but qualifies it with the imperative for action. In morality, in Gandhi's view, is reflected the entire being of a man, and his liberation—as the liberation of the whole humanity.

Gandhi's ultimate ideal of egalitarian communitarianism rests on the above assumption of human perfectibility and the individual's potential for virtue, goodness, truthfulness, nonviolence, and even 'Godliness'. Gandhi's individual is neither the atomized, material creature of the liberals nor the abstract, trans-empirical 'self' of Indian metaphysics. Gandhi's conception of the individual and the 'self' is concretely, communitarian, in both material and moral sense.

Gandhi was conscious of the difficulties in the journey to absolute/universal truth through relative truth of the individual. As a scientist, he felt the need for appropriate means for the purpose. Gandhi found Patanjali's five spiritual *yamas* (vows) particularly relevant and transformed the traditional symbolism of *vratas* (vows) into the political categoricals of liberation. He imaginatively extended the five *yamas* into an eleven-fold code of conduct (*Ekadash Mahavrata*) for the *Satyagrahis*. Gandhi lost no opportunity in improvising the contents of the vows and meaningfully using the popular faith for the national cause.

Not only this, Gandhi also expropriated the appeal of the heroic mythological icons for political and social objectives. His repeated references to the legendary figures such as Rama, Krishna, Prahlad, Harishchandra as incarnations of truth, love, devotion, righteousness bear this out. Images of Sita, Damyanti, Draupadi and Meera were also invoked as exemplars of resoluteness, nonviolent courage and voluntary suffering. Self-suffering was elevated as a political value and self-realization as a philosophico-political corollary of national liberation. Gandhi was absolutely convinced that a person's ability to rise in protest was ultimately dependent on his 'inner urge' for freedom. He attempted to reawaken this 'inner urge' through an imaginative politico-cultural symbolist strategy. For him, moral regeneration of the individual was coextensive with social and political regeneration of the nation.

Thus, Gandhi used the past but did not stop with it. He borrowed symbols from the scriptures, epics, mythologies and tradition but only to the extent, they served the transformative objective. Any symbol that militated against moral sense, social justice, truth/reason was unacceptable to him. An incessant seeker after truth and an unceasing experimenter, Gandhi constantly improvised traditional symbolism to suit the radical ends. That made his symbolism dynamic, though it always remained focussed.

What is of most valuable salience for contemporary political theory, is Gandhi's innovative enunciation of key political symbols, rooted in a specific historical, politico-cultural context but rife with transhistorical and transcontextual implications. *Swaraj*, *Sarvodaya*, *Swadeshi*, Oceanic Circles, *Satyagraha*, *Samabhava* were conceptualized and concretized in clear political terms along with a big range of explanatory, supplementary and supportive symbols. *Swaraj* was conceptualized as the architectonic symbol. *Sarvodaya* was visualized as the egalitarian communitarian utopia. *Swadeshi* was a logical corollary of *swaraj*. Protest was enjoined as the highest duty, as *swadharma*, even as *dharma*. *Charkha* and *khadi* symbolized national self-respect and urge for self-reliance and economic freedom. Boycott was projected as an extended political form of the virtue of non-attachment. Burning of foreign goods (bonfire) was explained with reference to the popular myth of *Holika Dahan*, celebrating triumph of truth over untruth. In concrete political terms, it signified the sacred *yajna* of national liberation. It was also a specific form of assertion of national identity. The entire strategy of *satyagraha* was a symbolist strategy of political *karmyoga*. In its foundations, it was a trans-political mode of protest, with remarkable political results. Part of its success may be attributed to an exceptionally innovative delineation by Gandhi. The key political symbols ingeniously devised by Gandhi, far from being 'symbolic', are central to his philosophy and praxis, in terms of political ideals, vision, strategy of communication, articulation, mobilization and communion.

Gandhian symbolism may, thus, be seen as a historically-situated political strategy as well as a trans-historical vision, with larger theoretical and praxiological implications. It is signally significant as an alternative worldview, premised on Indian philosophy and tradition, yet transcending civilizational confines, in its universal humanist concerns. It is as relevant in theoretical discourse as in political praxis. Its integral perspective compels reconsideration of the existing paradigms of theoretical understanding and strategies of political and social transformation.

Notes

1. *Young India*, June 26, 1924, p. 210.
2. Norman Jacobson, "Political Science and Political Education," *American Political Science Review*, 57, 3, September 1963, pp. 561-569.
3. See for details, Michael Oakeshott, *Rationalism in Politics*, New York, Basic Books, 1962.
4. Michael Walzer, "Philosophy and Democracy," *Political Theory*, 9, 3, August 1981, pp. 379-99.
5. *Note 4.*
6. Marx's comment is relevant to recall in this context: "Criticism does not remain within itself, but proceeds on to tasks for whose solution there is only one means-praxis. Revolution without criticism is blind, criticism without revolutionary praxis is impotent." Karl Marx, *Critique of Hegel's "Philosophy of Right"* (A John and J.O. Malley *Trans*), Cambridge, Cambridge University Press, 1970, p. 137.
7. Jawaharlal Nehru, *The Discovery of India*, (1946) New Delhi, Oxford University Press 1981, p. 101.
8. Radhakamal Mukerjee, *The Way of Humanism: East and West*, New Delhi, Academic Books, 1968, p. 198.
9. Barrington Moore Jr. *Social Origins of Dictatorship and Democracy*, Boston, Beacon, 1966, p. 486.

10. Y.G. Krishnamurti, *Gandhism for Millions*, Patna, Pustak Bhandar, 1949, p.3.
11. Hannah Arendt, *Men in Dark Times*, New York, Harcourt, Brace and World, 1968, pp. 11-12.
12. See Alasdair MacIntyre, *After Virtue*, Notre Dame, University of Notre Dame Press, 1981, pp. 103-113.

3

Swaraj
The Architectonic Symbol

> "Let there be no mistake about my conception of Swaraj... at one end you have political independence, at the other the economic... It has two other ends. One of them is moral and social, the corresponding end is *dharma*, i.e., religion in the highest sense of the term... Let us call this the square of Swaraj, which will be out of shape if any of its angles is untrue."[1]

Swaraj is the architectonic symbol in Gandhian vision and praxis, personated in both individual and collective consciousness and political struggle. As much inward as outward, an imperative obligation and an inalienable right, a mode of self-realization and a vision of commonweal, *swaraj* has been conceptualized by Gandhi as a philosophy as well as a strategy of total transformation and emancipation. The vision is radical as well as rooted. It is idealistic as well as programmatic, historical as well as futuristic. *Swaraj* is truly the *summum bonum* of Gandhian philosophy and activism.

Swaraj, as an architectonic vision and symbol in Gandhian thought, is comparable to Plato's conception of *dikaosune* (justice) in the *Republic*, both epitomizing the interactive unity of the self and society on the one hand and of politics and ethics on the other. Plato had urged that humans should love and value material existence even though it be a distorted reflection of the 'eternally beautiful idea.' The innate beauty is imperishable. It is identical to the highest idea, which in turn, is a synonym of 'goodness'. It is an ineluctable duty of man to invoke 'beauty' and, thereby, both the highest idea and goodness. Goodness embodying idea and beauty, is in Platonic conception the *demurge* (the principle of creation), underlying everything in the mortal world. An intrinsic unity of beauty-idea-goodness at individual and collective levels signified justice in the ideal state of republic. Correspondingly (though not identically), Gandhi sought truth (*Satyam*) for purposive and integral welfare of humanity (*Shivam*), and upheld goodness as supreme beauty (*Sundaram*). At an abstract level, the architectonic symbolism of *swaraj* was meaningfully conveyed by the Vedic ideal of *Satyam, Shivam, Sundaram*. Gandhi valued more than anything else the beauty, along with the challenges, of the living material universe, a replica of the eternal beauty of absolute truth, conceived as God. Whereas in the Platonic ideal state, one had to be a philosopher in order to attain the commonly unattainable beauty, in Gandhian *swaraj*, a seeker after truth identified himself with his fellow-beings and sought to attain the bliss' epitomized in commonweal and collective effort.

Conceived simultaneously as the supreme objective and a comprehensive strategy, the multiple implications of *swaraj* are interspersed throughout the corpus of Gandhian writings. At one level, *swaraj* is Gandhi's answer to the British imperialism, at another it is a rejection of the entire paraphernalia of modern western civilization, at yet another level, it is an alternative worldview and a vision of emancipation of the individual, the nation and also the world. *Swaraj* is, thus, freedom from the imperialist yoke, exploitation, social evils, violence, inequality, injustice and fear of death. It is also self-government, substantive democracy, decentralized-humanized economy, a non-violent order, *Ramraj, sarvodaya* and globalism. The spinning wheel and *khadi*, Hindu-Muslim unity and anti-untouchability crusade, prayer and fasting, non-violence and truth and above all self-suffering and renunciation—all symbolize *swaraj*, at various levels and in variant situations. *Swaraj* is, thus, an integral perspective, historically contingent but not dated. Though primarily and rightly addressed to the situational problems of political subjugation, economic exploitation, cultural defeatism and social powerlessness, Gandhi's Swarajist perspective was, truly, far ahead of his times.

Etymologically, *swaraj* is a sacred 'Vedic' word, meaning self-rule and self-restraint and not freedom from restraint, which 'independence' is often taken to represent.[2] Since, individuals as well as nations are potentially capable of self-rule, in Gandhi's view, "political is no better than individual self-government". Accordingly, political self-government is attainable "by precisely the same means that are required for individual self-government or self-rule."[3] The obligation of the initial step towards *swaraj*, therefore, is vested in the individual, in Gandhian framework. *Swaraj* for a nation is axiomatically "the sum total of the Swaraj of individuals,"[4] comprising the nation.

Also, in Gandhian view, political self-government of the people is not merely external, but inclusive of the 'inward freedom' of the individuals. Gandhi qualifies it as a process of "reform from within".[5] The process is also a striving for self-perfection through rigorous self-discipline. Self-confidence and fearlessness are corresponding attributes of faith in God and truth and self-suffering. "Those who defy death are free from all fear"[6] in Gandhi's view. It is the evolution of 'inward freedom', manifest in 'inner voice' or conscience that, in fact, ensures the kingdom of God within, for Gandhi, as for Tolstoy. Gandhi's collective endeavour for *swaraj* is, therefore, coupled with his efforts to harness the innate capabilities of men and women for goodness, Godliness and virtue in service of the national cause. Politically translated, Gandhi's faith in the infinite potential of man (and woman) amounted to accepting individual as an end in himself, but a simultaneous acceptance of the philosophy of *advaita* inclines the Gandhian argument in favour of communitarianism, rather than individualism, as understood in the west. He clarified: "I value individual freedom, but you must not forget that man is essentially a social being. He has risen to the present status by learning to adjust his individualism to the requirements of social progress... Willing submission to social restraint for the sake of the well-being of the whole society enriches both the individual and the society of which one is a member."[7]

Aspiration for self-government is a moral duty (*dharma*) of the individual, as of the nation. In Gandhian persuasion, it is the performance of duties that entitles the individual for rights. Gandhi is confident that an individual, conscious of his duties, "will not yield to the tyranny of circumstance or system and dedicate himself to the ideal ends."[8] And, a nation comprising such individuals will have *swaraj* as an inalienable right, axiomatically. Hence, Gandhi's emphasis on individual *swaraj* as a corollary of national *swaraj*, although in the given historical context of imperialist subjugation, the latter was the immediate, imperative goal. The Indian freedom movement was, therefore, conceived by Gandhi as a step in the direction of *Purna Swaraj*. Accordingly, the content and the character of Indian nationalism was meaningfully transformed. The most distinctive feature of this transformation was the entry of the masses in large numbers in the struggle. It was Gandhi's ingenuity to portray *swaraj* in the symbolist terms of a *dharma yuddha* (a righteous war) for the common masses of rural India and to call for their participation in the same, as their *dharma* (a righteous duty). This was one of the levers of the multi-class, multi-caste national movement that he was able to build.

Gandhi, like Vivekanand earlier, had tremendous faith in the 'infinite power' of the Indian masses. Inhering unrecognized spiritual power, the Indian masses in his view, had the potential of combating the 'material tyranny' of the colonizers. What was needed was an imaginative effort at articulating and coordinating their diverse wills and activities. The colonial rule in India was based not merely on overt political power but on a comprehensive ideology of hegemony with significant psycho-cultural implications. On the one hand, the myth of 'civilizing the natives' was propagated and on the other, the pre-existing economic structure was calculatively destroyed. The 'self-image' of 'benevolent Raj' was also carefully publicized. The Indian society, under the colonial domination, was partly awe-stricken and partly terrorized. The hegemony was total, omniscient and omnipotent. To counter the formidable enemy, Gandhi devised *swaraj* as the counter-hegemonic overarching strategy matching the omniscience and omnipotence of the colonial hegemony, in both its 'inclusiveness' and 'aggressiveness.'

Gandhi tirelessly explained that an oppressive system was perpetuated not so much by repressive mechanisms as by the tacit consent of the oppressed. Protest, therefore, was obligatory. It was *swadharma* (moral duty), a divine dispensation, as it were. Why were the people not protesting? Gandhi found the answer, again, in the dehumanizing politics of colonialism. The awe-stricken and the terrorized people had been drained of their dignity, courage and self-esteem. *Swaraj* was to be the strategy to restore lost prestige, esteem, courage and confidence of the people. "Faith in one's own self" was equated by Gandhi with faith in God. Union with the fellow-beings was another manifestation of the same spirit. Invocation of the familiar image of *Daridranarain* to convey the message of serving the poor, as manifestation of divinity was an ingenious secular extrapolation of religious symbolism. The prime objective was to awaken, articulate, organize and unite the diverse sections of the masses to challenge the 'evil' empire and to make them believe that they could do it, within historical experience. *Swaraj*, as portrayed to them by Gandhi, symbolized both their aspirations and concerns.

Explaining his specific preference for the term *swaraj*, Gandhi stated: "Swaraj is an all satisfying goal for all time... our goal at any rate may be known by an indigenous word understood of the three hundred millions. And we have such a word in Swaraj first used in the name of the nation by Dadabhai Naoroji. It is infinitely greater than and includes independence. It is a vital word. It has been sanctified by the noble sacrifices of thousands of Indians. It is a word which, if it has not penetrated the remotest corners of India, has at least got the largest currency than any similar word."[9]

Initially articulated by the nineteenth century Renaissance thinkers, notably Raja Ram Mohan Roy, the democratic urge for *swaraj* was concretized in political terms by the early (liberal) nationalists and the revolutionaries, during the first two decades of the twentieth century. The critique of imperialism and the nationalist struggle had already become a force to reckon with, by this time. It was, however, under Gandhi's leadership that the 'democratic aspirations' were articulated as the 'common man's aspirations' with a sort of final realization that the British regime, far from being a historical agent of progressive change, as had been their claim since mid-nineteenth century, was, in fact, the chief obstacle to its attainment, owing to its imperialist designs and what Dadabhai Naoroji had presaged as "the unBritish rule in India". Accordingly, Gandhi visualized the Indian struggle for freedom as a composite striving for *swaraj*, which was broader than both political independence and formal democracy. Political independence was a prerequisite for the longer journey of *Purna Swaraj*, envisioned as all-round development of all (*sarvodaya*, in an ultimate sense). Struggle for independence was, thus, both a crusade for democratic rights and a preparatory ground for prospective *swaraj* as 'substantive democracy'.

It was in *Hind Swaraj* that the first conceptual enunciation of *swaraj* was attempted by Gandhi in terms of an alternative worldview and the ultimate ideal. The enunciation was a radical denunciation of the western-modern civilization as 'Satanic', ushering in a Black Age,[10] through its expression in comforts, possessions, fast locomotion, automation of work, mechanization and commercialization of life and erosion of ethical values and social norms. And, since in his view, India was "being ground down not under the English heel but under that of modern civilization"[11], outright rejection of the latter was imperative for real *swaraj*. *Swaraj* was also to involve the process of returning back to the roots, even though the process included a painful confrontation with the hazards of "progress, retrogression, reforms and reactions."[12] As *swaraj* had been lost, in the first place, owing to the failings of Indians themselves, it could be won back by rectifying the same. Therefore, he exhorted: "It is Swaraj when we learn to rule ourselves.... But such Swaraj has to be experienced by each one for himself."[13] Thus, both personal regeneration and national liberation were to compose *swaraj*, integrally, through a unity of ends and means and through commitment to truth and non-violence. Accordingly, *swaraj* was not merely political independence but also freedom from social, economic and political oppression by Indian hegemons. Hence, Gandhi's plea for a comprehensive agenda of transformation, in order to get nearer *swaraj*.

Gandhi's uncompromising emphasis on the constructive programme as a parallel movement along with the independence movement should be perceived as a carefully deliberated long-term strategy aimed at transforming the socio-cultural attitudinal universe in consonance with genuine *swaraj*. In his view, generation of social energy burnished by an ethical-social vision, through involvement of the people in a common cause, was to be the sure foundation of a participative political structure, where men and women would not be constrained by physical coercion, economic domination, political power and social repression. For Gandhi, the substantive implication of freedom was self-rule, that further implied moral duty, self-restraint and not freedom from all restraints which 'independence' was generally seen as implying,[14] in the Anglo-American liberal tradition. Further, *swaraj* in Gandhi's framework connoted qualitative change, that is, "change in the character of the rule and not merely of rulers."[15] The 'change' would remain superficial unless "the poorest shall feel it is their country in whose making they have an effective voice."[16] The true hallmark of *swaraj* of Gandhi's vision, therefore, would be "self-rule by the millions"[17] and mobilization of "the entire physical, economic and spiritual resources of all people in the service of the common good of all.[18] If Gandhi refused to distinguish between political expediency and personal morality, it was due to his concern for absolute standards.[19]

Ideally speaking, Gandhi was a philosophical anarchist and rejected State in all its forms in his ideal order of complete non-violence. His supreme objection to state power was its innate "violence in a concentrated and organized form" from which it could never be weaned.[20] However, perils of 'a-political' implications of the 'stateless', 'powerless', moralistic-anarchist vision of the ideal *Ramraj*, were ingeniously averted by Gandhi through enunciation of the sub-ideal, that is, a predominantly non-violent state. A political realist as he was, Gandhi realized that since conditions were not ripe for *Purna Swaraj*, insistence on immediate abandonment of the state machinery and related institutions such as parliaments, railways and fast transportation, doctors, lawyers, machinery and armed forces would be misplaced, though he always considered them as 'necessary evil' and would have welcomed their natural destruction. However, he still maintained that true *swaraj* would be possible only when violence is abjured by people and misuse of authority resisted through *satyagraha*.

This was in keeping with his basic argument in *Hind Swaraj*. His clarification, offered at a later stage (in 1946), is of particular pertinence: "There remains the question, whether, in an ideal society, there should be any or no government. I do not think, we need to worry ourselves about this at the moment. If we continue to work for such a society, it will slowly come into being to such an extent, that the people can benefit by it. The Euclid's line is one without breadth, but no one has so far been able to draw it and never will. All the same, it is only by keeping the ideal line in mind that we have made progress in geometry. What is true here is true of every ideal."[21] Accordingly, 'complete independence' in his view "will be complete only to the extent of our approach in practice to truth and non-violence."[22] He, therefore, urged people to carry truth and non-violence to the legislatures, so that they could carry out the popular will in earnest and work for commonweal. Though Gandhi was aware of the fact that "A government cannot succeed in becoming entirely non-violent," he still believed "in the possibility of a predominantly non-violent society."[23]

In 1921, Gandhi declared that his personal endeavour in the direction of the ultimate ideal of *Ramraj* notwithstanding, his corporate activity was "devoted to the attainment of Parliamentary Swaraj in accordance with the wishes of the people of India".[24] But, the parliamentary system was accepted by him as the available 'provisional system', preceding a more perfect system that would ensure power for the masses. Parliamentary Swaraj was defined as "the Government of India by the consent of the people as ascertained by the vote of the largest number of the adult population... who have contributed by manual labour to the service of the state and who have taken the trouble of having their names registered as voters."[25] Although Gandhi was not enthusiastic about institutional paraphernalia, he was, nevertheless, concerned about the practice of values in social life and the probable role that institutions could play in this regard. He underlined the importance of judiciary and free press and separation of the judiciary from the executive for ensuring fundamental civil liberties and rights of the citizens. He also advocated adult franchise and decentralization of political authority as instruments of empowerment of people. However, an accompanying proviso for effective democratic governance was "the acquisition of the capacity by all to resist authority when it is abused."[26] This involved "educating the masses to a sense of their capacity to regulate and control authority."[27]

Thus, Gandhi's conception went far beyond the structural parameters of institutional democracy and envisaged an interacting, communitarian democratic dynamics between individuals and groups, and civil society and the state. Congnizant of the institutional and operational antecedents of democracy in the west, Gandhi was categorically against imitating western models: "They have systems suited to their genius. We must have ours suited to ours."[28] This vital insight of Gandhi was woefully disregarded at the time of the framing of the constitution for independent India and also in the subsequent course of democratic governance in the country, just as his advice—for non-violent defence or for re-training the police force to suit a genuine democratic order or for disbanding the Congress to allow Lok Seva Sanghas to grow in its place—had been rejected earlier.

Gandhi was aware and staunchly critical of the effective dissociation of the *demos* from the process of democratic governance in the west. He argued that a "superficial study of British history has made us think that all power percolates to the people from parliament. The truth is that power resides in the people and it is entrusted for the time being to those whom they choose as their representatives."[29] It is worth recalling that following the French Revolution, when the democratic experiment was carried out in the form of parliamentary democracy, the very principle of delegation of individual choice and individual sovereignty got institutionalized as 'representation' through an electoral mechanism. Henceforth, people began to exercise their sovereignty by surrendering it from time to time, as M.N. Roy characterized the process. This was probably the beginning of the basic contradiction of democratic theory and practice, resulting in complete mythicization of the concept of *demos*, thus, further distancing democratic governance from its root (Greek) meaning.[30] Gandhi remained a strong critic of the western parliamentary system not only for its mythicization of individual sovereignty but also for its incapacity to ensure freedom, equality and justice.

Gandhi warned against the oligarchic manifestations that mediated democratic governance in representative democracies in the name of "rule of the people", even though in effect robbing them of their social and moral content. In his view, the very essence of democracy is that "every person represents all the varied interests which compose the nation. It is true that it does not exclude and should not exclude special representation of special interests but such representation is not its test. It is a sign of its imperfection."[31] True, 'mass democracy' was on the ascendancy owing to irreversible historical forces. The 'centralized state' was the logical, inevitable result of the forces that were at work in industrial capitalist-liberal societies in the west. Gandhi admitted that "most people do not understand the complicated machinery of the government... (yet) every citizen silently but nonetheless certainly sustains the government of the day in ways of which he has no knowledge."[32] Therefore, he wanted the state "to carry out the will of the people, not to dictate to them or force them to do its will."[33]

His chief objection to the centralized state, as mentioned earlier, was its innate violence. In 1925, he argued that the "people of Europe have no doubt political power but no Swaraj.

Asian and African races are exploited for their partial benefit, and they, on their part, are being exploited by the ruling class or caste, under the sacred name of democracy.... Shorn of all the camouflage, the exploitation of the masses of Europe is sustained by violence."[34] Accordingly, he castigated not only the liberal but also the socialist varieties of democracies as both had created potential 'Leviathan' (s), though with varying ideological justifications, legitimized in the name of 'people'. Centralization was the logical outcome of the industrial civilization, in Gandhi's view, expressive in both expansive state and gigantic economic structure. Centralization breeds as well as rests on violence. Hence, Gandhi's advocacy of a decentralized democracy with a 'predominantly non-violent state', with least centralized governance and an economic structure operating through need-based small-scale and cottage industries, 'appropriate technology' and a non-objectified relationship with nature. This, in his view, will increase the sphere of individual freedom by minimizing both state-power and violence. For him, "centralization as a system is inconsistent with a non-violent structure of society."[35]

Redefining democracy as "the rule of unadulterated non-violence,"[36] Gandhi reasoned that "the nearest approach to civilization based upon non-violence" was "the erstwhile village republic of India."[37] This was a notable illustration of self-government for him, where each individual was related to political authority by immediacy of interest. It is pertinent to note that Gandhi is not alone in invoking the past as a corrective to the present. Similar attempts have also been made in the west, though with a difference. Whereas Gandhi is absolutely sure and convinced of the desirability and feasibility of the ancient Indian republican institutions, notable disagreement persists among western theorists on the possibilities of the Golden Age of the republican tradition.[38] In Gandhi's view, the essence of democracy will truly manifest in self-sufficient, self-governing villages in which voluntary cooperation would be the condition of dignified and peaceful existence,[39] as it had been in the past. It was through the system of *panchayats*, Gandhi reminds us that the organic character and continuity of Indian society and culture had been preserved in the face of foreign intrusions and onslaughts. In this structure, composed of innumerable villages, Gandhi visualizes "ever widening, never ascending circles". The outer circumference in this structure "will not wield power to crush the inner circle but will give strength to all within and derive its own strength from it."[40] Such a transition will not be complete without the participation of people at large, at every level of decision-making.

Thus, in Gandhi's vision of true democracy "life will not be a pyramid with the apex sustained by the bottom. But it will be an oceanic circle whose centre will be the individual, always ready to perish for the village, the latter ready to perish for the circle of villages, till at last the whole becomes one life composed of individuals never aggressive in their arrogance but ever humble, sharing the majesty of the oceanic circle of which they are integral units."[41]

Gandhi cautions against centralized authority that "does the greatest harm to mankind by destroying individuality which is at the root of all progress and insists that individual should be the basic unit of the decentralized democratic political structure."[42] The individual of Gandhi's conception, however, is not the atomistic, isolated and self-maximizing individual of the market society, but the interacting, participative human-individual with a sense of belonging to his surroundings. The above Gandhian assertion transcends the western liberal-capitalist-democratic political discourse that tends to neglect the social basis of individual political activity.

At the second Round Table Conference, Gandhi proposed an indirect scheme of elections. In 1942, he reiterated that seven hundred thousand villages of India would be restructured according to the will of its citizens, thus decentralizing power among seven hundred thousand units. For, real democracy in his view, could not be built from top to bottom but from 'bottom upwards'. Guided by the norms of social, civic and political responsibility, voluntary cooperation, and participatory culture, decentralized democracy would produce real freedom and ensure equality. The government of the village will be conducted by the panchayat of five persons annually elected by the adult villagers, male and female, possessing minimum prescribed qualifications. These will have the authority and the jurisdiction required but they will not rule 'over the people'. Panchayat rule will be truly "people's rule". Since, there will be no system of punishment in the accepted sense, the panchayat will be the legislature, judiciary and executive combined to operate its year of office.[43] Physical force will be replaced by 'truth force' in the Panchayat Raj.

The non-violent democratic state of Gandhi's vision is conceived as a secular state,[44] and the magnanimity of the majority and the willingness of the minority to yield to the majority is solicited for harmonious social life and ordered political life.[45] He did not fail to underline that the "rule of the majority has a narrow application, i.e., one should yield to the majority in matters of detail. But, it is slavery to be amenable to the majority, no matter what its decisions are... Under democracy individual liberty or opinion and action is jealously guarded... What we want, I hope, is a government not based on coercion even of a minority but on its conversion."[46] As mentioned earlier, the state in Gandhian conception is a mere means, not an end. The ultimate end of the non-violent state is to advance, "the greatest good of all." But as the state is rooted in violence, in a predominantly non-violent society, the state will govern the least and use the least amount of force.

It is noteworthy that Gandhi's conception of "the least governance" is not synonymous with the laissez-faire philosophy of negating the negatives. Gandhi also visualizes a positive, constructive role for the decentralized political institutions, beginning with the panchayats in all spheres —economic, social, political—in the democratic structure of his dreams, primarily with a view to setting right the balance in favour of the individual.

As mentioned earlier, Gandhi's Panchayat Raj ensures that no interests are excluded from the governing process, and contentious issues are resolved through dialogue. Effective checks on the power of sinister interests are constituted through the moral authority of the community. In his view, since "Truth did not admit of violence being inflicted on one's opponent, ... he must be weaned from error by patience and sympathy."[47] Citizens are provided opportunities to pool their information and insights, deliberate together, criticize each other's ideas and arrive at collective decisions. The very process of political participation will make citizens feel 'responsible' for their political actions as well as for the consequences. It will also heighten awareness of their true interests as well as a 'communitarian' concern for the well-being of fellow beings. "Evolution of democracy" in his opinion, "is not possible if we are not prepared to hear the other side... If intolerance becomes a habit, we run the risk of missing the truth."[48] Gandhi, like Plato, visualizes a harmonious political universe, where the 'self' is coterminous with society and also with polity. For Gandhi, however, the central concern is not merely 'universal' but 'equal' participation and that is better ensured in a decentralized participative structure. Gandhi's envisioned democratic structure is, thus, more 'inclusive' and egalitarian than the Greek polis.

In Gandhi's decentralist order, of utmost significance is the corpus of norms of interpersonal cooperation, self-restraint, self-sacrifice and self-reliance as opposed to the modes of self-maximizing, self-centred and expansive manouvres in modern state apparatus. Gandhi has reiterated time and again that centralization is inconsistent with non-violence, as it inevitably cripples individual initiative and creativity and also the capacity to resist tyranny. In this context, Thomas Pantham has rightly commented that "Gandhi made an inversion of the Hobbes-to-Lenin approach to political theorizing. He based his theory and practice of democracy on a realistic, integral conception of human nature, which, while not denying man's selfishness, acknowledges his potential for rationality and goodness."[49] A decentralist order, as it logically functions through the smallest micro unit, actually operates through interpersonal interaction in contradistinction to the imposing corporate structure of depersonalized authority. The contradictions of communities/identities and state-power inhibiting the centralized state system, is resolved through the organizational principle of Oceanic Circles.

Thus, the Oceanic Circle model of decentralized democracy seeks to set right the 'inverted pyramid' of existing western democratic system standing on its head and to reset it on its base, the task of broadening the base and the top layers suitably architectured into the basic structure. It is in this counter-directionality that Gandhi's innovative significance lies.[50] The alternative model is designed to reinstate the *demos* rendered powerless by centralized state apparatus, and to restore the 'humane' displaced by the technicist, expansive economism. The model, as explicated by V.R. Mehta with reference to Aurobindo's paradigm, also envisages autonomous wholes rather than secluded, hierarchical, institutional structures.[51]

In the contemporary context, Gandhi voices his apprehension when he states that though democracy is a great institution, it is also liable to be greatly abused in the absence of commitment to a clear set of moral values in public life. Therefore, in his view, the remedy is "not avoidance of democracy but reduction of possibility of its abuse."[52] How to reduce the possibility of abuse? Gandhi suggests several means, that are pertinent even today. Joan Bondurant, in this context, rightly points out the significance of *satyagraha* and the limits of Liberal Democratic Theory, specially bearing upon the question of ends-means relationship and an adequate technique of action as distinct from the structure of political machinery. She states that the "premier technique for adjusting conflicting interests" in the western liberal democratic states is "the unrefined method of compromise. Should the representative majority system by subverted, the ultimate remedy lies with violent revolution." It is when conflict persists that the Gandhian technique of "satyagraha supplies the process whereby constructive solutions may yet he achieved. Satyagraha points directly to a new method of revolution."[53]

For Gandhi, *satyagraha*, of course, is "the inherent right of a citizen" and also the most potent and successfully tested political weapon, capable of countering coercion and repression of utmost intensity. It is at the same time an imperative obligation, to be undertaken not recklessly, but with absolute sincerity and self-discipline. Self-government, in Gandhi's view, "depends entirely upon our internal strength, upon our ability to fight against the heaviest odds."[54] The 'ability to fight' also involves, what he calls 'inward freedom' that is, "reform from within".[55] That is the moral foundation of *swaraj*. In this sense, *swaraj* is "the sum total of the Swaraj (self-rule) of individuals. And such Swaraj comes only from performance by individuals of their duty as citizens."[56]

Gandhi regards personal *swaraj*—as self-discipline for both the rulers and the ruled---as an imperative pre-condition for genuine democracy. Transparency in governance, especially in matters of finance, can be ensured through articulate public opinion, acting as a persistent vigilant force. Indeed, for Gandhi, political power is as much a 'trust' with the rulers in a decentralized polity as wealth is in the economy of his conception. The rulers are expected to work as the 'trustees' of the people in a democracy, not as 'self-declared guardians' as Robert Dahl describes them. Resurrection of the *demos* through participative democratic structures is, thus, both an ethical imperative and a political agenda for *swaraj* in the Gandhian alternative.

Equally significant is Gandhi's emphasis on "continuous effort to be independent of government control."[57] Gandhi's prolonged experiments in constructive programme are of specific relevance in this context in terms of both mass awareness of the social weaknesses and their redress through self-help and cooperative, collective effort as well as preparedness of ordinary, common people for great sacrifices for a worthy cause. For, democratic governance, in Gandhi's views, is not merely a structural arrangement of rights but also a normative concern with civic and political obligations.

Going beyond the structural parameters of institutional democracy, Gandhi envisages a truly interactive reciprocal democratic dynamics. Quest for autonomy and freedom is also simultaneously a quest for equal rights, though inevitably accompanied by equal obligations. David Held, in a different context, delineates autonomous citizens as "free and equal in the determination of the conditions of their own lives, so long as they do not deploy this framework to negate the rights of others."[58] Citizens in the Gandhian republic are not only 'externally' autonomous as postulated by David Held but also 'internally' free, as mentioned earlier. This, notably is a 'non-instrumental' view of human beings in society, marked by freedom from fear and coercion, domination and exploitation of all kinds. Gandhi's decentralized order is predicated on the understanding that active participation of all is the condition of optimum development of each, in both political and moral terms. Politics, in this sense, assumes the status of a redemptive, moral activity for Gandhi, as for Rousseau or Aristotle, earlier.

Ultimately, Gandhi's oft quoted but most disregarded 'talisman' of judging all politico-economic decisions and actions by the criterion of their relevance for the poorest sections of society, provides the supreme ideal for a democratic polity, worth aspiring for.

Political *swaraj* would be incomplete without economic *swaraj*. The essence of economic *swaraj*, as of political *swaraj*, is equality, justice, space for individual creativity and non-violence. Gandhi perceived a non-violent system of government to be "clearly an impossibility so long as the wide gulf between the rich and the hungry millions persists."[59] Therefore, economic equality was the master-key to what he visualized as 'non-violent independence'. Since, the seeds of violence lay in gross economic inequalities, eradication of the same through non-violent means was essential for economic *swaraj*. Hence, Gandhi's unqualified stress on comprehensive economic restructuring to be accomplished through a human-ethical approach. This would involve a total transvaluation of the prevailing western-materialist worldview and a rejection of its attendant industrial-capitalist infrastructure. Economic *swaraj* of Gandhi's vision would be approximated through his ethico-economic strategy comprising adherence to bread labour, voluntary restriction of wants, *swadeshi*, simple/appropriate technology and trusteeship.

In his incisive indictment of the exploitative and oppressive, utilitarian and dehumanizing core of the modern, western urban-industrial, capitalist civilization, Gandhi rejects all varieties of 'economism' that hurt the moral well-being of an individual or a nation, as 'immoral'.[60] At the same time he also postulates that "all true ethics to be worth its name must at the same time be also good economics."[61] Indeed, both ethics and economics are grounded in identical human realm of necessity/freedom for Gandhi. However, accepting ethical and spiritual values as superior to materialistic greed, Gandhi disfavours the modern industrial centralized economic gigantism. It is important to remember that Gandhi does not reprove the 'west' as such, but the attitudinal and normative aspects of the aggressive, acquisitive industrial capitalist economy that have characterized it.

What makes Gandhi's critique most radical is the fact that it penetrates not only the roots of what he calls "the disease of the industrial capitalist system of production, consumption and control but also its psyche and the normative universe."[62] As mentioned earlier, for him "true economics stands for social justice", in contradistinction to that which "enables the strong to amass wealth at the expense of the weak"[63], both within nations/states and on the global plane. He was equivocal in stating: "Industrialization depends entirely on your capacity to exploit, on free markets being open to you and in the absence of competitors..."[64] Therefore, in his view, moral decline of the individual and society parallels the material civilizational progress, when market tends to replace the bonds of family, tradition, community and nature. The severed bonds need to be resurrected to redress the balance of the social universe.

Gandhi's principal objection to the industrial capitalist productive system is its indiscriminate production of commodities irrespective of the 'felt' needs of the people or a society, 'profit', not 'use', being the primary objective. Gandhi's argument is both pragmatic and normative. As profit-oriented, unrestrained commodity production necessitates not only large-scale production, but also centralization of the means of production and accumulation of capital, exploitation and violence inevitably accompany industrial growth. Voicing his variance with Jawaharlal Nehru on the issue, Gandhi categorically stated that the evils were inherent in industrialism, and no amount of socialization could eradicate them.[65] Hence, his plea for a decentralized economy, envisioned as 'exploitation-free' and non-violent and conducive to *swaraj*. Interestingly, Marx's conceptualization of man's alienation from nature, from his species-beings, fellow-beings and his own-self,[66] appears to be in close proximity with Gandhi's disavowal of forced labour, misconceptions of leisure, and concentration of wealth.[67] The goal of economic activity, in Gandhi's view, is to provide work for body and to satisfy the basic needs of all. Economic progress with the above objective would be moral progress as well. In the Gandhian economy, then, 'happiness' would be understood in terms of 'contentment' and bread labour would not only guarantee full employment but also guard against the excesses of overproduction and underproduction.

Gandhi understood the nefarious implications of the nexus of economic and political power, exemplified by the liberal-capitalist state in the west not only in terms of concentration of politico-economic resources but also distribution of the same in society, at large. Citing the American example, he argued: "the most industrialized country in the world, and yet, it has not banished poverty and degradation. This is because it neglects the universal man-power and concentrates power in the hands of the few who amass fortunes at the expense of the many".[68] Gandhi urges for 'equitable distribution', if not 'equal distribution', which is a higher ideal and seemed remote in the given context. In his view, "Adam Smith's pure economic motive constitutes the principal 'disturbing factor' in modern civilization that has got to be overcome".[69] Extension of the same principle to the global level has resulted in imperialism, as discussed earlier. Gandhi, therefore, is most vociferous in rejecting 'economics that permits one country to prey upon another' as 'immoral'.[70] As the British rule had allied India with international capitalism, it was logical for Gandhi to denounce the trans-national ventures of ambitious imperialists.

On philosophical plane, there is no ontological dualism

between the realms of 'necessity' and 'freedom' in Gandhian discourse. The question specifically centres on the notion of 'basic' needs. Acquisition of wealth is, in any case, immoral for Gandhi. He would like wealth to be used only for fulfilling the basic needs and for nothing more. The basic needs of a man, in his view, ought to be determined by his "natural needs", inclusive of "... a balanced diet, a decent house... facilities for... education... and adequate medical relief." Comparatively viewed, Herbert Marcuse's discrimination of 'true' and 'false' needs is of particular pertinence in the contemporary context, which is characterized by simultaneous attainments of corporate developmentalism and loss of self-hood.[71] 'Freedom' and 'self-hood' indicating the discriminating capacity of judging the order of needs is also the prerequisite of *swaraj*, again applicable to both individuals and nations. *Swaraj* is as much 'inward' as 'outward' in philosophico-spiritual sense, and as much 'individual' as 'national' in a politico-economic sense. It is the ultimate criterion of human development for Gandhi.

Therefore, he urges to retrace steps "from the demoralizing industrialism" to stop "going downhill in the path of progress" in both economic and moral terms.[72] His alternative to reorganize the economic order on the decentralist principle visualizes self-dependent units "bound together in bonds of mutual-cooperation and interdependence", proposing self-sufficiency itself as "a kind of service"[73]. The idea of self-sufficiency is strongly qualified by Gandhi by the doctrine of *swadeshi* and the imperative of fulfilment of basic necessities, precluding both a parochial notion of self-contained economy and a parasitical economy surviving on outside support. His exhortation for voluntary restriction of wants is a social expression of his ethical precept of *aparigraha* (non-possession). The precept emanates from the core values of truth and non-violence and enjoins the denial of things, not essentially needed by a person.

The question of limitation of wants has been a major point

of controversy and criticism. Gandhi has been flayed for wanting to keep the people in perpetual poverty and demanding ascetic austerity from them. However, his insistence would appear meaningful if weighed against the growing realization of the dangers of what has been described as 'hypercommodification', exhaustion of natural resources and scaring proportions of pollution. Gandhi's warning that earth has provided enough for everybody's need but not for anybody's greed is echoed by the contemporary critiques of reckless "objectification of nature".[74] His concern with recycling materials was taken to be an obsession by his contemporaries and the modernists, but, if we look at it from the long-term view of what J.C. Kumarappa called the "economy of permanence", 'the obsession' is decipherable as a carefully thoughtout idea. The built-in compulsive tendency, in modern industrial infrastructure, of maximizing growth and long-term planning, makes it imperative that the people be induced to buy more goods than they actually need. Consequently, consumer goods become not only associated with social status but also with a misconceived notion of self-expression. Gandhi regards these as superfluous, even undesirable, and hence his stress on regulation of wants.[75]

In Gandhian economics, restriction of wants is coupled with economic equality and individual and social welfare. For the purpose, Gandhi advocates comprehensive redistribution of the economic resources of society by "levelling down of the few rich" and a "levelling up of the semi-starved naked millions". This would facilitate transformation towards a non-violent society, through reinforcing the ideal of 'contentment'. Accumulation of wealth is theft by this criterion.

Consumer society is the inevitable result of the capitalist-industrialist model of development and the resultant conflict between economic and social/moral values. Threats to the environment, the ecology and the minimal well-being of the deprived two thirds of the world, are the inevitable consequences of the aforesaid model. With a sixth of the world population residing in the affluent North, consuming a major part of the non-renewable resources and energy available on earth, enough will not be left to fulfil even the basic needs of the rest of the world's population in foreseeable future. In the context of the Club of Rome's call for "zero growth", what is really needed to redress the balance is decisive reduction in the level of consumption specially in the developed west (North), as urged by Gandhi.

Gandhi was particularly apprehensive of market mechanisms aptly described by Sukhumoy Chakravarty as "a good servant but a bad master". He, therefore, redefined economic activity in terms of 'service' to one's fellow men. He insisted that economic activity is to be carried out not for maximizing one's own profits, but to serve the interests of the society as a whole. That is also the crux of *swadeshi.* It is not 'essentialism', exclusiveness, isolation or non-involvement with the rest of the world, as is sometimes misconstrued. It is a plea for subordination of self-interest to social good, and for simplicity and development of individual creativity. Gandhi visualized cooperation between the primary units leading to an integrated national economy and the establishment of a global economy based on mutual cooperation, on terms of equality. He even pointed out that it was against the *swadeshi* spirit to try to produce goods that could not be produced in one's own area or country without extraordinary effort. But, Gandhi emphasized that economy, national or global, would be equitable and just only when it had its roots in communities where human values such as "selfless service and ahimsa" that were to animate it, were nurtured.[76]

Gandhi's argument, as V.K.R.V. Rao has rightly commented, was the logical extension of "his economic thinking that frowned upon industrialism and urbanism and sought to make man rather than the machine the prime instrument of production."[77] It was a crusade against what Herbert Marcuse described as "the transformation of natural world into a technical world."

That brings us to the most debated issue of our times, namely, the issue of the role of technology in contemporary civilization. To begin with, Gandhi's critique of machinery, currently termed as technology, is philosophically rooted in his ideal of bread labour (minimum physical labour). The critique is a serious confrontation with the formidable problem of violence, centralization of power, unemployment and what is now being termed as "jobless growth" on the one hand, and "objectivization of man", on the other. The essence of bread labour is the simultaneous recognition of the 'human-self' and non-exploitation. In Gandhian enunciation, if everyone keeps the minimum of his earnings (through bread labour) for his basic requirements and contributes the rest to society, concentration of wealth in a few hands and the consequential inequality, exploitation and injustice would automatically end. Probably at a deeper level, Gandhi was concerned with arresting the process, described by Heidegger as the "objectivization of needs as goals". He saw technology not as a neutral instrument but as instrumental in enhancing the capitalist hegemony "of the few at the expense of the many."[78] Marcuse, to an extent, echoed Gandhi when he argued that technology had replaced ontology in industrial civilization and that its ever-increasing capacity of domination was a matter of grave concern.[79]

For Gandhi, technology was a also a manifestation of violence, not only in terms of destructive machinery, but also in terms of concentration of resources, privilege and monopoly, and the exploitative use to which these were put.[80] As large scale production and clever marketization of consumer goods reifies needs, it also homogenizes choice and quantifies creativity. Technology no longer remains a simple instrumentality. The discerning alternative that Gandhi visualized was a decentralized economy, with a real possibility of harmonizing cottage and big industries if the latter were so planned as to help the villages.[81] He also pleaded for simpler, alternative forms of technology, and a more judicious use of science, in consonance with nonviolence.[82] Needless to state, such technology would be essentially non-repressive. This was a non-instrumental view of both man and nature that Gandhi so vociferously advocated as a possible rectification of both 'scientistic' epistemology and industrialist-capitalist economy. The view has been reinforced by the growing skepticism regarding the efficacy of technological apparatus in solving the problems of dehumanization, pollution, ecological imbalance etc., that are, to a large extent, the outcome of the successes of the present model of growth, development and modernization.

Thus, translated in political terms, *swaraj* is self-determination and self-rule, in economic terms, it is self-reliance and economic justice. It is a synonym of honourable existence for both individual and nation/state. *Swaraj* is also an inalienable right (and a *swadharma*) for individuals and nations alike. Gandhi would urge for a redefinition of the very objectives of the enterprise of development/progress/modernization and consequently a recasting of the strategies to achieve the objectives in keeping with his 'talisman' of judging the validity and desirability of a political or economic act/decision by its possible impact on the poorest segments of society. That would be reinstating the 'humane' in place of a 'commercial' criterion.

A Swarajist redefinition of the objectives of the present development syndrome would involve some basic questions, such as: ultimately what is the objective? Who are the real beneficiaries? What are the costs? Who suffers most? How is the pie distributed? Identification of appropriate strategies would depend upon the answers one gets for the above questions. The primary task of the Swarajist endeavour would, thus, be to make people aware of their 'true' interests as against those projected to be such by the dominant/ruling classes. Gandhi is convinced that if the mode of production, instead of being centralized in a few hands, is scrupulously decentralized, the issue of 'social costs' vis-a-vis the contemporary growth model can be resolved. Further, effective regulation and ultimate disintegration of the centralized politico-economic power, may facilitate emergence of a form of humanized technology in the service of society, to combat 'unfreedom' in all forms.

An essential presupposition underlying Gandhi's visualized scheme of development is that each individual should attain a measure of economic *swaraj* so as to have some measure of impact on the economic activity at the larger level. At the same time, Gandhi also makes the point that the potential of each individual for economic productivity is coupled with the needfullness of voluntary interdependence with his neighbours, thus, enhancing the process of formation of broader units, self-reliant as well as interdependent. The appropriate production-strategy is conceived by Gandhi as labour-intensive not capital-intensive, empowering the human 'hand' and precluding both gigantism and exploitation. As non-exploitative economy is the *sine qua non* of elimination of privilege, it is conducive to a non-violent, equitable order.

A liberated society will be intrinsically moral for Gandhi. No action is moral which is not voluntary. An action dictated by fear or coercion of any kind would be violent and cease to be moral.[83] True democracy or genuine *swaraj* is marked by freedom from fear and coercion in every sphere of life—social, political, economic, and at all levels—individual, national and global. Ahimsa is the greatest force at the disposal of mankind in Gandhi's view.[84] It is, indeed, the true element of life and also the highest *dharma* (duty) in the service of both *swaraj* and humanity. He, therefore, rejects the juxtaposition of individuals and nations regarding the pursuance of non-violence.[85] Given the logic of the convertibility of means and ends, violent means must result in violent ends. Judged so, the moral society envisaged by Gandhi is an ideal, markedly in dissonance with the existing reality. While Augustine found in the reality of "moral man in immoral society" a source of pessimism, the possibility and the potential of the moral man was a matter of conviction for Gandhi. He was assured that the immoral world could be redeemed and intrinsically transformed, in actuality, into a moral one, that is, a good society.

In Gandhi's view, no one could lead an integrally religious/moral life without identifying himself with the whole of mankind. This was not possible in contemporary times without participating in political and economic action.[86] Thus, politics is a redemptive activity for Gandhi and economics, embracing the material basis of the "good of all". And, purposive participation in both is a signal value. It is a righteous duty of every citizen and of every nation to resort to Satyagrahic non-cooperation, whenever honourable existence or self-respect is hurt.[87] Foreign help and ideologies, he emphasized, must be accepted only to the extent to which they could be assimilated to the national scene.[88] Gandhi's insistence, it would seem, is on discriminating choice. Choice does not imply intervention in every act of decision-making but an opportune defiance of structures of control. Gandhi's definition of non-cooperation as refusal to cooperate with the exploiters on their own terms[89] is, in fact, addressed to the deeper dimensions of *swaraj*. Though not a determinist, Gandhi was convinced of the evolution of human civilization towards *ahimsa*, as a progressive realization of the values of dignity, equality, community, and justice.

Swadeshi is another foundation of *swaraj*. It is pertinent to note that the vow of *swadeshi* among others that the inmates of the Satyagraha Ashram at Sabarmati had to take, stipulated: "There is no place for self-interest in Swadeshi, which enjoins the sacrifice of oneself for the family, of the family for the village, of the village for the country and of the country for humanity." As instance of a progressive assimilation of smaller loyalties into the larger ones, *swadeshi* is an exhortation for 'disinterested'/selfless service of mankind, without merging one's identity.[90] *Charkha* (spinning wheel) and *khadi* (handspun cloth) represented what Gandhi described as "wholesale Swadeshi mentality and a foundation of economic freedom and equality." *Khadi* was the symbol of unity of India in Gandhi's own admission. It was characterized by Nehru as "the livery of India's freedom". *Khadi* was a summation of Gandhi's economic philosophy of "decentralization of the production and distribution of the necessaries of life."[91] Similarly, the message of the spinning wheel was wider than its circumference. It was of simplicity and service of mankind. In hand-spinning and hand-weaving Gandhi saw the secret of economic and moral regeneration of India.[92] It was also conceived as "a symbol not of commercial war but of commercial peace" and "of non-violent economic self-sufficiency."[93] *Swadeshi* is, thus, the foundation of *swaraj*, though it is also used as a synonym of *swaraj* by Gandhi at several places.

Defining *swadeshi* as the spirit of preferring to use and serve the closer surroundings as compared to the distanced ones, Gandhi urged to "make use of the indigenous institutions and serve them by curing them of their proven defects" in the political domain; and to "use only things that are produced by my immediate neighbour and serve these industries by making them efficient and complete where they might be found wanting," in the domain of economics.[94] *Swadeshi* therefore, is an argument in favour of a self-reliant national economy and a decentralized political structure. However, the concept is not exclusivist. It does not rule out, as mentioned earlier, 'inter-national' collaboration and cooperation, at both regional and global levels, with two preconditions: for things which can be produced locally, outside productive forces should not be allowed, and consumption of locally produced commodities should be preferred to the imported goods, and secondly, collaboration/cooperation between the interacting units should proceed on terms of equality. If these two conditions are met scrupulously, *swadeshi* and globalism can go together. The possibilities of regional cooperation are also intrinsic to the logic of *swadeshi*. *Swadeshi* as both "self-reliance and inter dependence on equal footing," provides a sound theoretical basis for a Gandhian agenda to combat the disriminatory practices.

Gandhi's life-long crusade against the industrial-capitalist economic order, perceived by him to be the root of all the contemporary ills, would remain incomplete without his doctrine of trusteeship that involves changes in the existing institutional arrangements as well as values. In Gandhi's own words, it is a "means of transforming the present capitalist order of society into an egalitarian one. It gives no quarters to capitalism but gives the present owning class a chance of reforming itself... does not recognize any right of private ownership of property... does not exclude legislative regulation of the ownership and uses of wealth... an individual will not be free to hold or use wealth for selfish satisfaction... the difference between... minimum and maximum incomes should be reasonable and equitable and variable from time to time, so much so that the tendency would be towards the obliteration of the difference... the character of production would be determined by social necessity and not by personal whim or greed.[95] Although Gandhi had clearly accepted the need for state-ownership of key industries in preference to private ownership, nevertheless, he remained apprehensive of the potential tyranny of the state: "if the state suppresses capitalism by violence, it will be caught in the coils of violence itself and will fail to develop non-violence at any time."[96] In fact, the state can destroy only possessions, not possessiveness, as V.K.R.V. Rao has aptly commented.[97] The ideal of trusteeship is, thus, conceivable in terms of a 'post-capitalist' and 'post-socialist' vision of economy and society.

Through trusteeship, Gandhi sought to overcome the evils of both private ownership and state enterprise. As mentioned earlier, he was averse to the former for its exploitative, inegalitarian, unjust core and the latter for its authoritarianism and violence. His own alternative envisaged a just economic order by voluntary conversion of the exploiting class, in favour of socio-economic justice through moral appeal to their conscience. He was convinced that what was needed was "not the extinction of landlords and capitalists but a transformation of the existing relationship between them and the masses into something healthier and purer."[98] The process would involve moral transformation of the exploiters on the one hand and realization of their own moral strength by the masses on the other. The latter was essential, as exploitation in Gandhi's view, ultimately depended on the cooperation of the exploited. Mutual recognition of each other's importance and needs by the conflicting classes, would lead to the establishment of moral equality between them.[99]

Thus, trusteeship does not rule out class-division, but certainly aims at overcoming class-conflict.[100] Gandhi's explanation rested on the teachings of the *Gita*, specifically, the ideals of *aparigraha* (non-possession) and *samabhava* (equability) which signified that everything "belonged to God and was from God. Therefore, the entire wealth of society was meant for his people as a whole, not for a particular individual. When an individual had more than his proportionate portion he became trustee of that portion for God's people."[101] "If this truth was imbibed by the people," he was optimistic that "trusteeship would become a legalized institution."[102] This would ensure an equitable order not only in India but on the global level as well.

Gandhi has been flayed vehemently, especially by Marxist

critics for allegedly providing a theoretical justification, through a spiritual pretext, for the perpetuation of private property and ownership. However, Gandhi's response to his critics (recorded in 1947) is notable for his integral perspective: "When Panchayat Raj is established, public opinion will do what violence can never do."[103] The argument reinforces his earlier argument in favour of *swaraj*, rejecting both expansive economy and powerful state as violent, and dehumanizing.

Gandhi's stress on people's power is unmistakable. "When the people understand the implications of trusteeship and the atmosphere is ripe for it, the people themselves, beginning with Gram Panchayats will begin to introduce such statutes. Such a thing coming from below is easy to swallow. Coming from above, it is liable to prove a dead weight."[104] The egalitarian order visualized through trusteeship is not one of "dead equality where every person becomes or is rendered incapable of using his ability to the utmost possible extent."[105] It is an order inspired by the *Ishopnishad* ideal of *Tena Tyaktena Bhunjeetha*, signifying dedication of all that one creates and possesses to the service of all for universal benefit.[106] Notwithstanding the inequitable distribution of material and mental resources among human beings, Gandhi was assured that men and women could act as trustees rather than as owners of their resources and could thus consider themselves as partners of their fellow-beings in society. Through such a radical redefinition of both the means and the ends of production, as Raghavan Iyer has commented, "Gandhi sought to lay the basis for a redistribution of wealth that would be consistent with a sacrificial moral order (*rta*) of the cosmos."[107] This could also serve as the basis of a fundamental reform of society.

As a votary of Ahimsa, Gandhi could not have subscribed to the utilitarian formulae of "the greatest good of the greatest number". In his view, it was a parochial doctrine of misconceived notions of human happiness and attainments. The negative fall-out of the politico-ideological implications of the doctrine was writ large on the face of Europe, he argued. As neither freedom nor happiness was quantifiable in terms of numbers, in Gandhi's view, the utilitarian precepts were antithetical to *swaraj*. *Sarvodaya*, the doctrine of "the greatest good of all" was his own alternative. It was a simultaneous assertion of human dignity and freedom as an end-in-itself. In Gandhian framework, freedom was inseparably accompanied by responsibility. He insisted that there was "not a single virtue, which aims at or is consistent with the welfare of the individual alone. Conversely, there is not a single offence which does not, directly or indirectly affect many others besides the actual offender. Hence, whether an individual is good or bad is not merely his own concern, but really the concern of the whole community, nay of the whole world."[108] *Sarvodaya*, in essence, is a vision of 'liberation of all' grounded in the 'liberation of the whole man'.

Moving beyond the utilitarian ethic, Gandhi redefined individual existence in terms of purposive social activity thereby ensuring the good of the individual in the good of all. This 'firm recognition of the moral priority of social virtue' to use Iyer's expression again, converted the individual's quest for 'happiness' into a quest for 'goodness' and *swadharma*. Fellowship and communitarian affability was but an extension of the mutual fulfilment of obligations, in the envisioned order. In *sarvodaya* society, the 'good order' was simultaneous with the 'good individual'.

Like Marx's communism, Gandhi's *sarvodaya* order was a classless, egalitarian, exploitation-free, non-repressive utopia comprising unalienated individuals, who would 'naturally' identify with nature, the human-species, the fellow-beings and one's own-self. That was humanism of a supreme order that the two shared, despite some fundamental differences in terms of conceptual framework and methods of revolution. Whereas the

Marxist model was thoroughly materialist and did not reject industrialism, the Gandhian ideal was inclusive of 'trans-materialist' aspects of human life and rejected industrialism on both economic and ethical grounds, although, his sub-ideal state, that is, "the predominantly non-violent state" was granted concessions in terms of limited industrialization". Here also, Gandhi's chief objection, as that of Marx, was not only to the unqualified concentration of resources in a few hands and the resultant exploitative apparatus but also to the deeper dimensions of acquisitiveness and greed. Gandhi, unlike Marx, saw the entire arrangement as a manifestation of violence. Hence, his remedy, again unlike Marx, was a non-violent decentralized politico-economic order, as discussed earlier. It is equally pertinent to remember that at variance with Marx, Gandhi's critique of industrial capitalism, as a historically situated argument was primarily a critique of the colonial politico-economic hegemony. Therefore, it was inextricably related with *swaraj*. Quest for social emancipation, in this sense, was as much a duty as struggle for political independence. Therefore, as has been rightly commented "the dreams about Sarvodaya and the focus on non-violence served the same goal."[109]

Sarvodaya rests on the assumption of human perfectibility and the individual's potential for virtue, goodness, truthfulness, non-violence and Godliness, as referred earlier. However, the concept of 'self' is not trans-empirical and abstract, primarily and absolutely, as is argued by several noted interpreters of Gandhi. It is concretely communitarian. It is notable that even the doctrine of *karma* is interpreted by Gandhi as granting adequate choice to the individual regarding performance of 'acts of goodness'. The individual himself, therefore, is the ultimate repository of moral responsibility for each of his acts. It is also notable that the abstract, trans-empirical idea of God is remarkably concretized by Gandhi and communicated to ordinary people in terms of truth, love, selfless action and *Daridranarayan*. There is no place for determinism of any sort in Gandhian thought and praxis. In Bandopadhyaya's apt observation, "the striving for self-perfection is the same as acquiring virtue, which stands for the qualities required for the attainment of the preconceived values."[110] Thus, *sarvodaya* would be unrealizable without the emancipatory ethic, at both individual and social ends.

In the Gandhian framework of ends-means equation, self-generated moral power is the most efficacious instrumentality of social transformation and real *swaraj*, through non-violent action, fraternity and *sambhava* on the one hand and selfless action (*nishkam karma*), on the other. It is in this sense that Gandhi argues in favour of the revolutionary potentialities of "the unarmed individual." Logically then, self-realization and quest for social justice form a composite urge for *swaraj*. Jaya Prakash Narayan shares Gandhi's emphasis on 'human reconstruction' as "an essential foundation for social reconstruction."[111] *Sarvodaya* would thus signify *swaraj* in its ideal condition, simultaneously libertarian and egalitarian and inescapably communitarian.

The ideal of *sarvodaya* is also symbolized by *Ramraj*. *Ramraj* is the supreme symbol of Gandhi's egalitarian-communitarian utopia, denoting an enlightened anarchy, politically manifest in "the sovereignty of the people based on pure moral authority."[112] In an ultimate sense, *Ramraj* symbolizes "God's kingdom on earth". The conception has been dubbed by several critics as retrogressive and "more conservative than the most conservative ideas". The critics, however, miss the pith of Gandhi's argument. Gandhi, as stated earlier, conceived of God primarily as an impersonal idea, translatable in truth, justice and service of the downtrodden, and not as a deity, historically located and conceptually confined. God realization, therefore, far from a synonym of insulated, individualized quest, is, indeed, a communitarian ideal and aspiration, in Gandhi's view.

Criticizing Gandhi's advocacy of resurrecting the ancient simple peasant communities, upholding the values of rural simplicity and moral integrity, it has been pointed out: "The *Ram Rajya* by which he [Gandhi] swore, was, if Valmiki, the author of *Ramayana* is to be believed, very far from being wholly agricultural---it was highly urban also, as is testified by Valmiki's description of Ram's Ayodhya, nearly as gorgeous as Ravana's Lanka."[113] The argument is refutable by the very fact that Gandhi far from being enamoured of the urban civilization, was its strongest critic, not for any idiosyncratic reasons, but because of its evident subversion of simplicity, integrity and communitarian bonds. The point of dispute, therefore, is not the urban/rural configuration but the set of values that are represented by each. Further, if Rama's Ayodhya is accepted as "nearly as gorgeous as Ravana's Lanka", Gandhi is, very clearly, not referring to it, as a historico-geographic entity. His allusion is not particularistic, but to the universalistic ideal of a non-exploitative, egalitarian-communitarian order. Therefore, by identifying Gandhi's *Ramraj* with the historical, mythological-scriptural version of *Ram Rajya*, we run the risk of missing the universalist elements in his vision.

Symbols from mythology or tradition are, admittedly 'restrictive' in important senses, yet when these are creatively transformed to transcend their given historical context by a gifted innovator like Gandhi, they 'reveal' and 'suggest' much more than their descriptive form. This is truly the case with the rich symbolism of *Ramraj* employed by Gandhi with a view to conveying to the Indian masses the true content of *Purna Swaraj* of his conception. And for this, he reiterated time and again that India had to be her 'own self', in civilizational terms, and resist the "on-rush from the West". It was only by being her 'own self', that she could contribute meaningfully to the larger humanity. Political *swaraj* was a stepping stone for the higher goal of *Purna Swaraj.*

It is notable that Gandhian conception of *swaraj* does not stop with the geopolitical boundaries of the nation-state. A persuasive argument in favour of an equitable, egalitarian and just 'inter-national' order, predicated on the values of dignity, autonomy and community, is clearly perceptible in his paradigm. Needless to state, the global order of Gandhi's conception would be non-violent, non-hegemonic world order pledged to what Glenn Paige has aptly described as 'global sarvodaya'.[114]

If 'global sarvodaya' is accepted as the ultimate objective, it follows axiomatically in the Gandhian logic that globalism would be coextensive with *swaraj*, understood as both the essence and the vision of liberation. It is a unitive vision born of spiritual communion and identification with all human beings, in fact, all living beings impelling him to state that 'if one man gains... the whole world gains with him and if one man falls, the whole world falls to that extent.[115] As stated earlier, metaphysically speaking, Gandhi's faith in the unity of mankind and universal brotherhood could be attributed to his faith in the Vedic conception of *advaita* accepting the entire cosmos as created by a single divine source. He gave it a modern, temporal content and translated it into a humanistic vision, of emancipating the individual as well as the global community.

Thus, *swaraj* is instrumental in "the realization of the greater mission of the brotherhood of man."[116] Gandhi could not visualize the rise of one nation on the ruins of other nations. "Not isolated independence but voluntary inter-dependence has to be the goal of world states,"[117] he assented. As mentioned earlier, interdependence is as much the ideal as self-sufficiency for both individuals and nations. That signifies the true significance of the Vedic ideal of *vasudhaiv kutumbkam* (the whole world is one family). *Swaraj*, in this sense, is freedom positively open-ended, consisting in progressive availability to others in loving service and sacrifice, and a foundation of globalism. Given the global reality of competitive power structures, Gandhi would insist on the values of love (*ahimsa* in true sense), community and sacrifice to be structured into human interactions at each level—from the family to the world, so that violence and exploitation could be realistically combated.

It bears repetition to stress that *swaraj* cannot be the foundation of globalism unless the present form of state-centric/market-centric global power-structure is reoriented in favour of 'communitarian values', as stated earlier. The formidable objective presupposes a reorientation of the state-power itself. Here, it is pertinent to note that though Gandhi's primacies are 'communitarian', the institution of State is accepted in his framework as a necessary (evil!) political unit in the existing global structure. The nature of the state (whether a 'nation state' or a 'nations-state'), however, needs to be transformed drastically.

Gandhian *swaraj*, in no sense, is narrow nationalism or chauvinism, but is "consistent with the broadest good of humanity at large". *Swaraj* is the foundation of globalism in this sense. Employing Plato's idiom it might be said that globalism, in essence, is *Swaraj writ large*. In other words, it is the underlying thread of integrality amongst the diverse nation-states in the world, not as isolated/antagonistic political units but as interacting partners in an equal relationship. In the 'inter-nationalist'/globalist world order of Gandhi's conception there is no place for impositions (interpreted as 'violent') of either political decisions or commerce upon an unwilling people.[118] It is pertinent to reiterate that Gandhi's objection is not to the 'foreign-ness' of a nation, or its ideas or products but to its exploitative, hegemonic even homogenizing trait. And, that he would vehemently urge to resist and combat, through articulated, non-violent protest, boycott, and non-cooperation and adherence to *swadeshi*.

Self-reliance with self-confidence is the *sine qua non* of *swaraj*, but so is a deep-rooted concern with humanity, in Gandhi's view. Nations/states not merely adorned with *de jure* sovereignty in external terms and formal representational legitimacy in domestic terms but personifying *swaraj* in both spheres, are capable of generating and sustaining a global order of justice, peace and equal human rights for all. True *swaraj* and globalism are *en rapport* in Gandhi's vision. The Swarajist-globalist vision of Gandhi is a vision of harmonious interaction, giving no quarters to 'clashes of civilizations', in any sense. The idea is best summed up in his own words: "... we will exploit none just as we will allow none to exploit us. Through Swaraj we would serve the whole world..."[119]

Thus, *swaraj* in Gandhian thought is truly architectonic, in terms of both conceptualization and political praxis. As an ideal, it is the emancipatory utopia of egalitarian communitarianism and as an agenda of transformation, the multifaceted struggle against oppressive structures of domination in all spheres and at all levels.

Notes

1. *Harijan*, January 3, 1937, p.374.
2. *Young India*, March 19, 1931, p.38.
3. *Young India*, December 1, 1927, p.402 and October 15, 1931, p.305.
4. *Harijan*, March 25, 1939, p.64.

5. *Young India*, November 1, 1928, p.363.
6. M.K. Gandhi, *Hind Swaraj*, Ahmedabad, Navajivan, 1989 (7th edn), p.74.
7. M.K. Gandhi, *Democracy: Real and Deceptive* (comp. R.K. Prabhu) Ahmedabad, Navajivan, 1961, p.32.
8. Y.G. Krishnamurti, *Gandhism for Millions*, Patna, Pustak Bhandar, 1949, pp.15-16.
9. *The Collected Works of Mahatma Gandhi* (hereafter, *CWMG*), Vol.35, p.456.
10. *Note 6*, p.34.
11. *Note 6*, p.30.
12. *Note 6*, p.82.
13. *Note 6*, pp. 58-59.
14. *Young India*, March 19, 1931, p.38.
15. *Note 6*, p.65.
16. *Young India*, September 10, 1931, p.255.
17. *Note 6*, p.68, and *Young India*, March 26, 1931, p.46.
18. *Harijan*, May 27, 1939, p.143.
19. R. Iyer, *The Moral and Political Thought of Mahatma Gandhi*, Delhi, Oxford University Press, 1973, p. 61.
20. N.K. Bose, *Studies in Gandhism*, Ahmedabad, Navajivan, 1962, p.202.
21. *Harijan*, September 15, 1946, p.309.
22. M.K. Gandhi, *Constructive Programme: Its Meaning and Place*, Ahmedabad, Navajivan, 1961, p.7.
23. *Harijan*, March 9, 1940, p.31.
24. *Note 6*, p.13.
25. *Young India*, January 29, 1925, p.41.
26. *Note 25*.
27. *Note 25*.
28. *Harijan*, January 2, 1937, p.374.
29. *Note 22*, pp. 8-9.
30. See Asha Kaushik (ed.), *Democratic Concerns: The Indian Experience*, Vol. I & II, Jaipur, Aalekh, 1994, Introduction.

31. *Note 7*, p.7.
32. *Note 7*, p.30.
33. *Note 7*, p.70.
34. *Note 7*, p.76.
35. *Harijan*, January 18, 1942, p.5.
36. *Harijan*, October 13, 1940, p.320.
37. *Harijan*, January 13, 1940, p.411.
38. See for details, Robert Dahl, *Democracy and Its Critics*, Delhi, Orient Longman, 1991, p.299.
39. *Note 37*.
40. *Harijan*, July 28, 1946, p.236.
41. *Note 40*.
42. *CWMG*, Vol. 59, p.319.
43. *Harijan*, July 26, 1942, p.238.
44. *Harijan*, September. 22, 1946, p.231.
45. *Harijan*, July 1, 1939, p.185.
46. N.K. Bose (ed.), *Selections From Gandhi*, Ahmedabad, Navajivan, 1948, pp.110-111.
47. M.K. Gandhi, *Satyagraha in South Africa*, Ahmedabad, Navajivan, (1928) 1993, p.6.
48. *Note 7*, p.34.
49. Thomas Pantham, "Thinking with Mahatma Gandhi: Beyond Liberal Democracy," *Political Theory*, Vol.II, May 2, 1983, p.176.
50. Asha Kaushik, "The Inverted Pyramid and Gandhi's Counter-directional Paradigm," *Political Science Review*, Vol.32, 1-4, January-December, 1993, pp.66-74.
51. V.R. Mehta, *Ideology, Modernization and Politics in India*, Delhi, Manohar, 1983, pp.180-88.
52. *Young India*, May 7, 1931, p.99.
53. Joan Bondurant, *Conquest of Violence*, Berkeley, University of California Press, 1967, pp.225-26.
54. *Young India*, December 1, 1927, p.402.
55. *Young India*, November 1, 1928, p.363.
56. *Harijan*, March 25, 1939, p.64.

57. *Young India*, August 6, 1925, p.276.
58. David Held, 'Democracy and the Global System' in D. Held (ed.), *Political Theory Today*, California, Stanford University Press, 1991, pp.228-29.
59. *Note 22*, pp.20-21.
60. *Young India*, October 13, 1921, p.325.
61. *Harijan*, October 9, 1937, p.292.
62. See Ramashray Roy, *Understanding Gandhi*, Delhi, Ajanta, 1996, pp.61-79.
63. *Harijan*, October 9, 1937, p.292.
64. *Young India*, November 12, 1931, p.355.
65. *Harijan*, September 29, 1940, p.299.
66. Karl Marx, *Economic and Philosophic Manuscripts of 1844*, Moscow, Progress, 1974, (4th edn.), pp.66-74.
67. See for instance, *Young India*, Oct. 15, 1931, p.310, and *Harijan*, Dec. 7, 1935, p.341, and June 29, 1935, p.156.
68. *Harijan*, March 23, 1947, p.79.
69. *Harijan*, September 21, 1934, p.253.
70. *Harijan*, August 25, 1946, p.281 and December 21, 1947, p.476.
71. Herbert Marcuse, *One Dimensional Man: Studies in the Ideology of Advanced Industrial Society*, Boston, Beacon, 1964, pp.5-7.
72. *Young India*, August 6, 1925, p.273, and *Speeches and Writings of Mahatma Gandhi*, Madras, Natesan and Co., 1933 (4th edn.) pp.353-355.
73. S. Jaju (comp.), *The Ideology of the Charkha*, Varanasi, Sarva Seva Sangh, 1951, pp.86-88.
74. See, for instance. Herbert Marcuse; *One Dimensional Man*, Boston, Beacon, 1964; William Leiss, *The Domination of Nature*, New York, George Braziller, 1972; and A. Wilden, *System and Structure*, London, Tavistock, 1972.
75. *Harijan*, February. 1, 1942, p.27 and February 24, 1946, p.19.
76. M.K. Gandhi, *From Yarvada Mandir* (trans. V.G. Desai), Ahmedabad, Navajivan, 1957, p.66.
77. V.K.R.V. Rao, *The Gandhian Alternative to Western Socialism*, Bombay, Bharatiya Vidya Bhavan, 1970, p.12.

78. *Harijan*, Nov. 2, 1934, pp. 301-32 and *Young India*, October 22, 1931, p.318.
79. See for Instance, Herbert Marcuse, "From Ontology to Technology: Fundamental Tendencies of Industrial Society" in S.C. Browner and D.M. Kellner, *Critical Theory and Society: A Reader*, New York, Routledge, 1989, pp.119-127.
80. *Young India*, June 17, 1926, p.218, October 13, 1921, p.325 and November 13, 1924, p.378.
81. *Young India*, November 15, 1928, p.381 and *Harijan*, November 16, 1934, p.316 and September 22, 1946, p.322.
82. Pyarelal, *Towards New Horizons*, Ahmedabad, Navajivan, 1959, pp.45-46. Also see, Kanu Gandhi (Comp.) *Swaraj Through Charkha*, Sevagram, All India Spinners Association, 1945, pp.5-6.
83. M.K. Gandhi, *Ethical Religion*, Madras, Ganesan, 1922 p.43. Also see *Young India*, May 25, 1925, p.178.
84. *Harijan*, July 20, 1935, p.180 and August 25, 1940, p.260.
85. *Harijan*, November 12, 1938, p.328.
86. *Young India*, June 18, 1925, p.214. Also see *Harijan*, September 9, 1924, p.298.
87. *Young India*, August 8, 1920, p.3.
88. *Harijan*, July 3, 1937, p.165.
89. *Young India*, October. 8, 1925, p.346.
90. *Note 76*, p.66.
91. *Note 22*, pp. 12-13.
92. *Young India*, September 17, 1925, p.321, and July 21, 1920, p.4.
93. *Young India*, February 8, 1921, p.406. Also see *Khadi: Why and How?* Ahmedabad, Navajivan, 1959, p.150.
94. *Note 90*.
95. *Harijan*, October 25, 1952, p.301.
96. Pyarelal, *Note 82*, pp.86-87.
97. V.K.R.V. Rao, *Note 77*, p.51.
98. N.K. Bose, *Note 46*, p.93.
99. *Note 46*, pp. 97-98.
100. *Note 46*, p.95.

101. *Harijan*, February 23, 1947, p.39.
102. *Note 101*.
103. Pyarelal, *Note 32*, pp.86-87.
104. *Harijan*, March 31, 1946, pp.63-64.
105. *Harijan*, February 22, 1942, p.49.
106. *Note 105*.
107. Raghavan Iyer, *Note 19*, p.14.
108. M.K. Gandhi, *Truth is God*, Ahmedabad, Navajivan, 1959, pp.123-24.
109. R. Ulyanovsky, *Three Leaders*, Moscow, Progress, 1986, p.33.
110. J.. Bandopadhyaya, *Social And Political Thought of Gandhi*, Bombay, Allied, 1969, p.67.
111. J.P. Narayan, *From Socialism to Sarvodaya*, Madras, Socialist Book Centre, 1956, p.17.
112. *Harijan*, January 2, 1987, p.374.
113. Bhagwan Das in S. Radhakrishnan (ed.) *Mahatma Gandhi*, 1944, p.75, quoted in Hiren Mukherjee, *Gandhiji: A Study*, Delhi, People's Publishing House, 1979, (3rd edn.) p.204.
114. Glenn D. Paige, "Gandhi's Contribution to Global Non-violent Awakening, "*Gandhi Marg*, 12,4, January-March, 1991, pp.429-443.
115. *Young India*, December 4, 1924, p.398.
116. *Young India*, June 18, 1925, p.211 and April 14, 1929, p.107.
117. *Young India*, July 17, 1924, p.236.
118. *Young India*, October 21, 1926, p.366, and April 4, 1929, p.107.
119. *Young India*, April 16, 1931, p.79.

4

Satyagraha
A Symbolist Strategy

> "It is certainly the *Bhagwad Gita's* intention that one should go on working without attachment to the fruits of work. I deduce the principle of *satyagraha* from this. He who is free from such attachment will not kill the enemy but rather sacrifice himself. Killing any enemy proceeds from impatience and impatience proceeds from attachment."[1]

Etymologically, *satyagraha* means "insistence on truth, and force derivable from such insistence". For Gandhi, truth is love and love is truth and "conduct based on truth is impossible without love." Truth-force, then, is love-force. Accordingly, Gandhi defines *satyagraha* as truth-force, love-force and soul-force.[2] Truth, also envisioned as God, signifies Godliness, virtue and goodness. *Satyagraha*, as political praxis could thus, be viewed as 'politics of truthfulness', instrumental in transforming the very nature of political activity and the public realm. Commensurability of end and means, ensured by conscious inculcation of the ethical conduct in the public sphere, is central to this transformative strategy.

Satyagraha, as a specific form of political praxis, is singularly distinguishable as, what we propose to designate, 'the symbolist strategy' of political revolution. The symbolist strategy, in

Gandhi's hands, operated through a dialectical unity of objectification and de-objectification of the subjective experience of individuals participating in public life. At one level, *satyagraha* was conceived as an endeavour in rediscovering and also authenticating the self in the public realm and at another, in socializing and collectivizing virtue in political praxis. Gandhi was convinced that as 'soul-force', the scope of *satyagraha* was broad enough to "take in every variety of wrong" and since the soul-force was as old as the world itself, its transformative credibility was trustworthy. *Satyagraha* was, therefore, conceived as a symbolist strategy, endowed with exceptionally efficacious 'communicative competence' for pragmatic political purposes. Consequently, *satyagraha* emerged as a novel experiment in political praxis in a trans-political mode based on a seemingly paradoxical synthesis of ethical idealism and political pragmatism, firmly rooted in the cultural symbolism of India's past and remarkably adapted to the requirements of a modern political revolution, specifically, in a colonial context.

It is notable that the idiom of symbols interposed in the cultural heritage of India, manifest in ancient mythologies, epics and scriptures and well-ingrained in popular consciousness was comprehended, reinterpreted and employed for political objectives by Gandhi, with a rare political insight and, on an unprecedented scale. In his ceaseless experiments, he rejuvenated several past religio-ethical images and ideals in new political forms and also introduced innovative symbols, necessitated by the contemporary objective conditions, suitable for the socio-political objective in view. It was due to Gandhi's extraordinary political astuteness and persistence that the plight of an exploited race (as in case of South Africa) and the agonies of a subject-nation (as in case of India) could get internationalized in politico-moral terms, at that moment in history. The uniqueness of *satyagraha* and its persistent use as an anti-colonial strategy was the prime mover in the above cause.

In all cases and in all its forms, *satyagraha* operated through exemplary ethics and determined action. It was the proper instrument for what Gandhi himself termed (in his *Satyagraha in South Africa*) a *dharma yuddha* (a righteous war) against the evil imperial empire. In a righteous war, there was no place for violence, hatred, falsehood or secrecy.

Truth is the cardinal core of *satyagraha* and non-violence its operative norm. The root meaning of truth is *sat*, which means 'being'. Nothing is, or exists in reality, except truth. Inevitably, *sat* as the 'eternal' is the only signification of God. And, where there is truth, there is also knowledge, which is true. Conversely, where there is no truth, there can be no true knowledge. That is why, as a complimentarity, knowledge, that is, *chit* is another attribute of God. Where there is true knowledge, there is always bliss, that is *anand*. And even as truth is eternal, so is the bliss derived from it. God is, therefore, identifiable in the trinity of the categoricals: *Sat-Chit-Anand* (truth-knowledge-bliss).[3] Howsoever variant the cognitions of God may be, for Gandhi the quintessence is in truth, in both transcendental and empirical senses. He was absolutely certain that "whatever we understand by God is implied in truth."[4]

Quest for truth is thus identical with the quest for God and transfiguratively with self-realization. In this regard, Gandhi specifically acknowledges his debt to the *Bhagwad Gita*, "as one of priceless worth". Since the individual self conceived in the *Gita* is a fragment of the 'Supreme Self', self-realization implies complete identification with the 'Supreme Self' and *ipso facto* with the entire cosmos as the manifestation of the Supreme Self. This would imply in Bal Gangadhar Tilak's words "knowledge of the identity of the *atman* with all created beings, that is seeing the entire creation embodied in oneself and seeing oneself embodied in the entire creation."[5] Gandhi's ingenuity lay in his translation of the metaphysical, ontological spirit of truth into a concrete ethico-political faith, borne out by his repeated assertion that he would but "...worship the God that is Truth or a Truth which is God through the service of (these) millions."[6] In Gandhian framework, therefore, individual self-realization is coterminous with collective-national (and even global) self-realization. Consequently, the aspiration to "become like unto God", culminates in 'Godliness' and is realizable only in selfless identification with the fellowbeings, and with, what he calls "the meanest of creation". Admittedly, Truth so realized is 'relative', but this is the surest path "to see the Universal and the all-pervading spirit of Truth face to face..."[7]

For Gandhi, mere 'perception' of truth had no special significance, unless inalienably accompanied by perseverance with 'speaking', 'upholding' and 'realizing' the same. This, in other words, implied a ceaseless, relentless and selfless pursuit of truth, also concurrently implying a resolve to eradicate false-hood, untruth, injustice and violence. The uncontested medium for realizing truth was *ahimsa*. The *Upanishadic* invocation—*asato ma sadgamaya*—("lead me from untruth to truth") did not amount to a clerical fiat for Gandhi but imparted an inspiring injunction for purposive praxis.

Gandhi, like Tilak, though with minor variance in explanation,[8] accepts *karmyoga* as the central message of the *Gita*,[9] delineating 'engagement in action' (that is, *karma*) as the supreme imperative of human life. Attainment of the aspired goal without requisite action is neither feasible nor desirable. He who gives up action falls, but he who gives up the lure of the reward, rises in *karmyoga*. Renunciation of the lure of the reward, in no way, implies indifference to the consequences. On the contrary, one is expected to anticipate the results likely to ensue from the undertaken course of action. In performing an act, what is of prime significance is not the certainty of the reward but perseverance of the endeavour in a selfless manner, detached from the predilection for the 'fruits' of the endeavour.

Such selfless, detached action is *nishkam karma*, a form of 'God-dedicated activity'.[10] *Karmyoga* is, thus, dedication of the individual Self to the 'Divine Self'. In the material-cosmic creation it is action performed in the spirit of renunciation of the reward. Interpreting the above injunction of the *Gita*, S. Radhakrishnan states: "The inevitable action has no binding power. Sacrifice itself is interpreted in a larger sense... The religious duty towards the Vedic Gods here becomes service of creation in the name of the Supreme."[11]

Gandhi insisted that the message of the *Gita* was not for the chosen few, the learned or the extraordinary beings, but for ordinary mortals. In his view, all are capable of comprehending and acting according to the 'message' of the holy book, admittedly, variantly perceivable. Disputing the argument that religion is antithetical to material well-being of the individual, Gandhi clarified: "The *Gita* has dispelled this (and) shown that... what cannot be followed out in day-to-day practice cannot be called religion."[12] The ideals of the *Gita*, in his view, could be practised by ordinary individuals (and society), although self-discipline and self-purification were essential prerequisites for the same. Gandhi tirelessly explained that the central message of the sacred text was voluntary renunciation of the desire for fruit. This was significant in terms of renunciation of the temptation for untruth or *himsa*. He was aware that it was a difficult precept, nevertheless, he was convinced about its attainability and efficacy. Accordingly, the supreme ideals of *sthitprajna* and of *anasaktiyoga* enshrined in the *Gita* were enjoined by Gandhi, as a form of spiritual preparation for political praxis. Those who had the will and the ability for the onerous discipline required for the national *yajna*, were endowed with the responsibility of performing *satyagraha*. For others, Gandhi translated part of the ideals in the form of *vratas* (vows) and exemplary ethics.

True, as C. Rajagopalachari asserted, the *Gita* was

"Gandhiji's *Shastra* and he acted according to its injunctions—work, detachment, prayer and surrender to God's will."[13] That was *karmyoga* transformed into *satyagraha* in the national struggle for freedom, elevating *anasakti* (selflessness) and *tapas* (self-suffering) as political values. Since man, according to Gandhi, "was neither mere intellect, nor the gross animal body, nor the heart or soul alone", physical, mental and spiritual purity was essential for harmonious working.[14] Self-purification, in the above-stated sense, amounted to attaining a stage of personhood "absolutely passion-free in thought, speech and action" as enjoined in the *Gita*. Urge for purification implied perfect realization of the *atman*, further implying self-restraint and self-discipline. In Gandhi's view, 'the evil within' could not be conquered until "we have reduced ourselves to nothingness". *Ahimsa* was the farthest limit of humility and a perfect vision of truth could only follow a complete realization of *ahimsa*.[15]

Gandhi warned against inertia being mistaken for humility. Conversely, it was the "most strenuous and constant endeavour entirely directed towards the service of humanity."[16] Employing his oft-repeated metaphor, Gandhi clarified: "There may be momentary rest in store for the drop which is separated from the Ocean, but not for the drop in the Ocean, which knows no rest... This restlessness constitutes true rest. This never-ceasing agitation holds the key to peace ineffable.[17] Such was the majestic grandeur of *karmyoga* as Gandhi comprehended it. The majestic grandeur was imparted through and imbibed in the political praxis to a large extent and with remarkable success. *Satyagraha* dawned as the most eloquent symbolist strategy of political revolution in the history of anti-colonial struggle.

Gandhi's profound faith in the doctrine of *anekantvad* or *syadvad* or the doctrine of 'manyness of reality' further strengthened his insistence on non-violence. As man was 'not capable of knowing the absolute truth', Gandhi stressed, he was 'not competent to punish'. In *satyagraha*, therefore, there was no room for force, coercion or violence in any form.[18] In this regard, Joan Bondurant rightly states that Gandhi's concept of truth, which is non-absolute, avoids the practical difficulty of ethical relativism through the introduction of non-violence as an operative principle of *satyagraha* in interpersonal relations and conflicts.[19]

By adopting *ahimsa* as the operative principle of *satyagraha*, Gandhi, in fact, accepted the socio-ethical criterion to judge truth in a given situation. As an objective idealist, Gandhi could infer intuitively that the individual's search for Truth operates in terms of the community or the social cosmos. "Truth and non-violence", were therefore, "not matters for mere individual practice, but for practice by groups and communities and nations."[20] Non-violence was "a social virtue to be cultivated like other virtues."[21] It was not merely a faith, but also a science, not merely an ideal, but also "a force which is self-acting."[22] *Ahimsa* vivified *satyagraha* in a true sense.

Gandhi's notion of *karma* was not deterministic. Man was the architect of his own destiny, in the sense that he had the freedom of choice, in terms of action. Of central significance in his *karma* syndrome was the 'manner' in which the aforesaid freedom was to be used.[23] Admittedly, the question of the 'manner' was not free from problems at either cognitive or practical level. However, Gandhi's unwavering answer was to follow the dictates of "the voice within".[24] Gandhi's rather positivistic firmness on the unfailing guidance of the 'inner voice' and its sanguinity has been a vexing irritant for numerous scholars and social scientists, who interpret Gandhian thought in rational-scientific terms. It is pertinent to recall Nehru's comment on 'inner voice':

> I knew that Gandhiji usually acts on instinct (I prefer to call it that than the inner voice or an answer to prayer), and very often

> that instinct is right. He has repeatedly shown what a wonderful knack he has of sensing the mass mind and of acting at the psychological moment. The reasons which he afterwards adduces to justify his action are usually afterthoughts and seldom carry one very far. A leader or a man of action in a crisis almost always acts subconsciously and then thinks of the reasons for his action. I felt also that Gandhiji had acted rightly in suspending civil resistance. But the reason he had given seemed to me an insult to intelligence and an amazing performance for a leader of a national movement.[25]

Admitting digression, it is notable that the 'intuitive phenomenon' has been a subject of study among philosophers, scientists and psychologists, for long. The thesis advanced by early rationalists was developed into philosophical conceptions that found their logical completion in conclusions directly opposed to the intentions of confirming the power of reason. Edmund Husserl, for instance, starting from the recognition of the impossibility of synthesizing rational thought with sensory experience, tried to build a 'pure logic' of scientific knowledge, banishing sense data from the sphere of consciousness. Excessive concentration on the mind's capacity for direct judgement of truth, typical of the early rationalists, led to conceptions of 'intuitionism' and the associated attempts to bring subconscious factors to the fore in the cognitive process. One of the most prominent advocates of intuitionism, Henry Bergson, considered man to be capable of learning the secret of being without any mediating link, even forms of the logical level of knowledge (reasoning, abstraction, generalization). Mind directly contemplated mind without any intermediaries. In intuition there was an indivisible and substantatively continuous flow of inner life.[26] The very fact of the protracted dispute between sensationalists and rationalists, and the difficulties associated with its resolution, witnessed the qualitative difference between feeling and reason, surmised to some extent intuitively and not capable of easy exposition in scientific terms. Gustav Bergmann explained that truths that are related to facts cannot be outside experience but analytical statements belong to the inexperienced. The difference between the two is grasped intuitively and is not created or dreamed up by philosophers.[27]

As highlighted by anthropo-psychological researches, intuition may have an extra-logical cognitive structure, though constitutive of consciousness. It is possible to explain the process. The mediating representations, arising historically, by linking the reflection of different phenomena in an interconnected whole according to a scheme of formal logic gave that scheme a certain content from the outset that reflected the really existing contradictoriness of the objective world. The content aspect of knowledge could now become a field in which the rational movement of thought was developed in formal logic. This field, in fact, determines the modes of thought at any stage of social development and the '*epistimes*' and the 'paradigms' (guiding principles of interpretation of the world) differentiate one worldview from another. The guiding principles fixed in consciousness with time may become so habitual that they are simply not noticed. In a way, consciousness gets liberated from them as a matter of course and passes into the sphere of the subconscious. To the extent a notion uniting different phenomena within the framework of some consistent scheme of formal logic may not, with abstraction from the content aspect of thinking, discover its presence in the logical scheme itself. An illusion is created consequently, that an act of imagination, in particular, 'intuitive prevision', expressed in a sudden 'dawning', 'insight', or 'guess', has a cognitive structure, extra-logical in principle.[28]

S. Radhakrishnan distinguishes between the "immediacy which appears at the sub-intellectual level (feeling) and the immediacy which appears at the supra-intellectual level (intuition)," the latter being "to some extent the result of discursive thinking." He further argues that "Plato and Shankara agree that... once the intuition is reached, it is prolonged into an intellectual ordering of images and concepts."[29] Thus, there is no break of continuity between intuition and intellect. In moving from intellect to intuition, one does not move in the direction of unreason, but enters the deepest rationality of which human nature is capable. Consequently, one thinks more profoundly, feels more deeply and sees more truly. One thinks with a certain totality, a specific wholeness.[30]

Gandhi's logic is self-explanatory: "When a man speaks of the 'inner voice', the scientists say it is auto-suggestion. It is auto-suggestion, indeed, because God is within... When the scientist speaks of the inner voice being auto-suggestion, he means to say it is the devil's voice. May be it is... God's voice is not heard in the heart of every person. It is no matter of inherent right. You must undergo a course of training, if you want to hear the voice of God."[31] Since 'inner voice' is the voice of God, it is, for Gandhi, the voice of truth *ipso facto*. Gandhi is categorical in his insistence that "just as for conducting scientific experiments there is an indispensable scientific course of instructions, in the same way strict preliminary discipline is necessary to qualify a person to make experiments in the spiritual realm... those who would make individual search after truth as God, must go through several vows.[32] Faith in 'inner voice' was, thus, not a spiritual facade for Gandhi, as was often alleged, but a 'true' and moral guide for practical political decisions. Upholding Gandhi's conviction Henri Brailsford commented: "Gandhiji did not plan it so, but in fact, the series of five struggles he led, wave after wave, with intervals for recovery in India and reflection in England, was the best strategy he could have followed."[33] Hence, the accusation that Gandhi arbitrarily postponed political action and withdrew movements, rather willfully in the name of 'inner voice', needs to be re-examined, in the above light, and with caution. If the conception of the 'inner voice' is taken as a symbolist persuasion, Gandhi's insistence on it explains the political sagacity underlying it.

It was employed, successfully, as a powerful moral sign to convey to the masses the righteousness of the struggle as well as the purity of means in the proposed struggle, a contention that could not be compromised at any cost. His political decisions justified in the name of 'inner voice', were primarily and pragmatically aimed at either ensuring a preparatory interval for the proposed struggle to be ensued at the opportune time or to purge the ongoing movement of unwanted *himsa*. In both cases, Gandhi's political sanguinity was clear.

In the realm of *satyagraha*, the symbolism of inner voice was also translated in terms of conscience, identified with the infallible voice of truth or God within. By upholding the sanctity of individual conscience, Gandhi assumed the omnipresence of the 'essential ethical core' in every human being and accordingly expected inevitable moral response from participants in the socio-political revolution. The conception of inner voice, translated as conscience, for the fellow revolutionaries and for the general masses, was thus used by Gandhi as a powerful moral deterrent to ensure purity of means in political praxis, on the one hand and to ensure political communication through a revered moral sign on the other. Raghavan Iyer has aptly commented that Gandhi was concerned with socializing the individual conscience rather than internalizing the social conscience.[34] However, if viewed in the perspective of Gandhi's ultimate social and human concerns, it would be amply evident that Gandhi was equally concerned with internalizing the social conscience. In fact, as mentioned earlier, there is no antithesis between the 'individual' and the 'social' forms and conceptions of goodness/oughtness in the Gandhian framework. The two interact in a reciprocal relationship, truly manifesting the spirit of *karmyoga*, that is, the service of humanity as the essence of 'self-realization'.

As mentioned earlier, Gandhi repeatedly insisted that just as for conducting scientific experiments there is an indispensable scientific course of instructions, in the same way strict preliminary discipline is necessary to qualify a person to make experiments in the spiritual realm. Everyone should, therefore, realize his limitations before speaking of his inner voice.[35]

The discipline of the vows, also stressed by Gautam Buddha and Mahavira, was systematized in the *Yogsutra* of Patanjali as five *yamas* (cardinal restraints), to be accepted as an indivisible whole, as the 'Mahavrata' and practised by an aspirant for God-realization and self-realization. This implied an absolute adherence to all the five *yamas*. If one was broken, all were broken. These five *yamas* were: *satya* (truth), *ahimsa* (non-violence), *asteya* (non-stealing), *aparigraha* (non-possession) and *brahmacharya* (celibacy/continence). Gandhi extended the five cardinals into eleven vows, the *ekadash mahavrata*, adding *abhay* (fearlessness), *aswad* (control of the palate), bread labour, *asprashyata nirakaran* (removal of untouchability), *sarva dharma samabhava* (religious tolerance), and *swadeshi*. The Vows were conceived by Gandhi primarily as the matrix of self-purification, self-discipline, character-building and what Richard Gregg described as "self-culture" at both individual and national levels. Extending the theo-cultural symbolism of the *vratas* (vows) as the essential prerequisite of 'self-realization' (as God-realization and as true salvation) to the political realm in terms of *Ekadash Mahavrata*, Gandhi sought to substitute the hegemonistic symbols propagated and popularized during the imperial domination by protest symbols at the level of mass-consciousness. For Gandhi, the struggle for *swaraj* was also a simultaneous quest for national identity, self-respect and self-reliance. Adherence to *Ekadash Mahavrata* could thus be relied upon as the solvent endowment singularly committed to the aforesaid national objectives. Gandhi was conscious of the popular faith in the *vratas* and lost no opportunity to harvest the same for the national cause.

It is often alleged that Gandhi's invocation of religious symbols and icons was essentially regressive. Surfacially speaking, any appeal to the past is regressive. In Gandhi's case, however, invocation of the past assumed a 'modern' political significance and served the purpose, not only of the nationalist struggle for freedom, but also a vision for the future. Indeed, in the Gandhian praxis, as mentioned earlier, theo-cultural symbols from the past were infused with pertinent political meaning and personated as living ideals. Gandhi was categorical on the unity of the moral and the political. He stated time and again that he could not be leading a religious life unless he identified himself with the whole of mankind and that he could not do so unless he took part in politics. Politics, by virtue of its imperative centrality in the given historical context, was a potentially redemptive activity. It was, thus, the concrete, supreme ideal of the service of the nation, that transformed the traditional symbolism of *vratas* into the political categoricals of liberation for both the individual and the nation. Gandhi employed the *vratas*, not only as a form of rigorous training in discipline required for *satyagraha*, but also for the generation of political will for independence. And, he was unprecedented as well as successful on both accounts.

When Gandhi emphasized: "Truth being that which *is*, can never be destroyed," with reference to the legends of devotees of God and truth, such as Prahlad, Harishchandra and Meera, he instantaneously brought home the message of the invincibility of *satyagraha* in the *dharma yuddha*, the righteous war against the alien rulers.[36] Since truth was conceived as 'reality' in an ultimate sense; secretiveness, evasiveness, deception, prejudice, exaggeration, adamance and even dogmatism were ruled out in the truthful struggle. The reality of truth, as reality in general, however, was not a 'finality' but a many-splendoured, ever-evolving, dynamic dialectic. In the political realm, the significance of Gandhi's distinction of absolute and relative truth lay in the political derivative of openness and open-endedness of his protest techniques. Gandhi's inclination for a realistic appraisal of the limitations of individual and group activity, despite faith in human perfectibility, could possibly be taken to account for his insistence on political cautiousness and gradual pursuance of social change.

If truth was "the highest law" for Gandhi, non-violence was "the highest duty".[37] The latter would become 'irresistible' only if implanted in mass-consciousness as the supreme "faith in the God of Love" and "infinitely greater than and superior to brute force".[38] Acknowledging his debt to the *Gita*, Gandhi elevated *ahimsa* to freedom from hatred, pride and anger, manifest in selfless action as God-dedicated activity or *karmyoga*. However, conscious of human fallibility vis-a-vis the absolutist conceptions of truth and non-violence, Gandhi also cautioned about the applicability of the twin concepts in varying situations, especially in a mass movement. It was probably in the above context that Gandhi made the distinction of *ahimsa* as a creed and as a policy in the freedom struggle: "If I had started with men who accepted non-violence as a creed, I might have ended with myself. Imperfect as I am, I started with imperfect men and women and sailed on an uncharted ocean... I could not have done otherwise if I was to introduce it into politics."[39] Cognizant of the difficulties of getting large masses to be non-violent in the exalted sense, Gandhi insisted on a limited number of adherents for direct *satyagraha*, often a small band of men—intelligent, honest and persevering who would ensure the requisite atmosphere for struggle on a larger scale.

In the strife-ridden context of India, with "Ravanas... warring with each other", as he portrayed the exploiters, Gandhi called upon the people to realize the strength of the philosophical injunction, *aatmavat sarvabhuteshu* (unity of the self with the entire creation) through adherence to *ahimsa*, negating *himsa* in all forms.[40] Active *ahimsa* in Gandhi's conception rests on *abhay* (fearlessness) and *tapas* (self-suffering)—the twin attributes of *karmyoga*. Accordingly, for the *satyagrahi*, *ahimsa* was neither the demonstration of physical strength nor the refuge of the weak but an expression of moral power of conscience, and resolute faith in the righteousness of the struggle as well as its ultimate invincibility. Gandhi was categorical that there could be "no such thing as non-violence of the weak."[41] To convey that violence was to be preferred to cowardice, if choice between the two was imperative, Gandhi evoked the ideal images of Rama, Krishna and Prahlad as against the evil incarnations of Ravana, Kamsa and Hiranyakashyap. The message went straight to the people as Gandhi had visualized: what was uppermost in the mass struggle was a firm, fearless, non-wavering faith in truthfulness and righteousness of the cause, and *satyagraha*, the weapon of non-violent protest was the most appropriate method of struggle.

For full realization of *ahimsa* in thought, speech and action, Gandhi recommended the ancient Indian discipline of *Brahmacharya*, signifying "conduct adapted to the search of *Brahma*, i.e., truth."[42] *Brahmacharya* is self-control in the complete sense. Rejecting the man-woman dichotomy in pursuit of continence, Gandhi sought to redefine and rechart the relationship of the sexes in Indian society, based on spontaneous discipline and self-restraint, paving the way for a social universe, free from repression and imposition and embellishing healthy companionship. *Brahmacharya* is not suppression of desires but absolute self-control, in Gandhi's view, "possible for any human being making the required effort."[43] Gandhi was, often, misunderstood on this point.[44] He was, nevertheless, firm that "without rule over the self there can be no *Swaraj* or *Ramraj*."[45]

The vow of *Brahmacharya* was inseparably related to the vow and practice of control of the palate (*aswad*), fasting and prayer. Gandhi believed that acquisitiveness, ostentatious vulgarity and insensate consumerism inevitably transform individuals into thieves. Therefore, he advocated the vows of non-stealing (*asteya*) and non-possession (*aparigraha*) enjoining the satyagrahis, not to "wish for anything which the meanest or the lowest of human beings cannot have."[46] Breach of this commitment only exacerbates human misery, agony and despair. Gandhi elevated the socio-moral content of *asteya* and *aparigraha* for ensuring individual rectitude as well as for probity in social life. Asceticism and self-denial assume socio-econo-ethical efficacy for very human reasons in Gandhian framework: "...the rich have a superfluous store of things which they do not need...while millions are starved to death for want of sustenance. If each retained possession only of what he needed no one would be in want and all would live in contentment."[47] Going a step further and rejecting the materialist utilitarian ethics, Gandhi reiterated that true civilization consisted not in the multiplication but in the deliberate and voluntary reduction of wants as discussed in the previous chapter. For him, 'reduction of wants' was not an urge for reversion to the primitive age, as often alleged, but a potential instrument to promote "true human happiness and contentment" on the one hand and to increase "man's capacity of service", on the other.[48]

The vow of 'bread labour', symbolized "the highest form of social service", paving the way to 'equitable' and ultimately to 'equal' distribution of resources in society.[49] *Swadeshi* was projected as a reminder of India's subjugation and presented as a potential strategy of politico-economic emancipation. The vows of *Sarva Dharma Samabhava* (equal respect for all religions) and 'removal of untouchability' were specifically addressed to issues bearing upon faith and belief systems of individuals on the one hand and social equality and justice on the other. The two vows were aimed at ensuring freedom of conscience for all and eradication of social discrimination. If the quest for *Sarva Dharma Samabhava* was inspired by the universal humanistic imperatives of *dharma*, the vow to reject untouchability was a penance for deliverance and dignity of the untouchables, designated by him as *Harijans* (chosen men of God). Gandhi's emphasis upon the aforesaid essentials was buttressed and strengthened by his call for 'fearlessness' (*abhay*), as the underlying substantive vow, metamorphosing abstract ideals into political praxis. *Abhay* (freedom from fear) signified the crux of dauntlessness, as exemplified in the *Gita*, as the prime requisite for *satyagraha*. Fear breeds cowardice which leads to violence and recourse to untruth. For Gandhi, therefore, *swaraj* presupposed abandonment of fear.[50] An unexceptionable *satyagrahi* as a fearless and equipoised (*sthitprajna*) *karmyogi*, would truly live up to the obligations of the national *yajna* of struggle for *swaraj* in Gandhi's envisioned strategy.

Ekadash Mahavrata was, thus, a profound and meaningful symbolist agenda ensuring inculcation of the 'self' into the public realm, transforming the apparently non-political, spiritual ideals into meaningful political motifs. In Gandhi's view, commitment to the cardinals at individual level would also elevate collective endeavour for *swaraj*. This does not mean that Gandhi was oblivious of human foibles and fallibility. He had the patience and the understanding to confront evolving challenges and every small step onwards was for him the source of added conviction and redoubled endeavour. Though uncompromising on the ultimate ideal, Gandhi was not dogmatic. A firm believer in *anekantvad* (manyness of reality), he was not unaware of the desideratum of manoeuvrability but was ever-insistent on creative experiments at ethical and political planes. Thus, as the Rudolphs have aptly commented, it was Gandhi's belief "that private morality had public consequences" and this reflected "the emphasis in traditional Hindu thought on ethical as against institutional restraints."[51]

The true strength of *satyagraha* lay in the spirit of *karmyoga*, the rigorous discipline of mind and body, elevating 'self-suffering' as a political virtue and 'self-realization' as a philosophico-political corollary of national liberation. For Gandhi, the ethical roots of the political movement were as significant as the movement itself. To the imperialists, "the conscious moral superiority of Gandhi and his followers was simply an additional irritation.[52]

Comparable to Spinoza's discipline of mind, Gandhi's ethico-spiritual discipline equipped him with both a comprehensive social understanding and a single-mindedness of the objective, without which achievement was impossible.[53] In *Hind Swaraj*, Gandhi wrote that rural India under colonial rule had, by and large, evaded the imperial legal and administrative institutions and the values of the cities. The common people still lived independently and followed their agricultural occupation. They enjoyed true Home Rule.[54] And, that was to be the model of true *swaraj*, in his view. In Gandhi's view, therefore, as mentioned earlier, the essential prerequisite for self-rule was the realization that it was unmanly and *adharma* to obey laws that were unjust. The struggle for freedom, thus, presented an opportunity for 'experiments with truth' as well. Thus interpreted, the 'political' was one of the facets of the collective-truth, unfolded, reformed and reformulated through *satyagraha*. The 'political', however, was also the 'central' in the given colonial situation. Gandhi's own explanation is pertinent in this context: "If I seem to take part in politics, it is only because politics encircles us today like the coil of a snake from which one cannot get out, no matter how much one tries. I wish therefore to wrestle with the snake." Symbolization of politics in the aforesaid manner signified, firstly the unavoidable reality of the colonial apparatus which was 'hegemonic' in content and methods, and, secondly, the necessity and the possibility of confronting and fighting the snaring and the oppressive 'hegemony'. Kripalani has rightly commented that if

Gandhi had been only a "good moralist but a defective or indifferent politician he would never have succeeded. The success then of his peculiar mission of spiritualizing politics depended largely upon his right political acumen and judgement... Gandhiji throughout his career, remained pre-eminently a good and astute politician and the Englishman knew this and feared him."[55] True, a mere saint or a recluse would have been conveniently ignored by the shrewd imperialists, but not the keen diplomat that Gandhi was.

Without falling prey to the convenient gambit of Mahatma versus politician, it is possible to perceive the integral unity of the 'spiritual moral', and the 'mundane political' in Gandhian thought and praxis, reinforcing and complementing each other. The struggle for *swaraj*, thus, symbolized both a quest for 'Truth-God-Virtue' and political independence. And in this quest, *satyagraha* was a radically novel experiment in creative political praxis. The imaginative and the successful fusion of the moral and the political has been aptly described as "Gandhi's version of this-worldly asceticism,"[56] with far-reaching political implications.

In terms of the objective conditions, it is pertinent to recall that when Gandhi arrived on the political scene of India, political activity was at a low ebb. The Congress, impoverished by the Surat split (1907) was falling short of the avowed objective of inspiring, enthusing or educating the people. The militant movement was being crushed by the imperialist regime. The communal virus had already started eating into the very vitals of the socio-political organism of India. The colonial repression had shattered and damaged the foundations not only of Indian economy and society but also the 'national psyche'. Gandhi set himself the task of transforming the ethos of despair with "a new voice in India's public life... with an urgency and a compulsion of conviction never encountered before."[57] He identified himself "with the masses of the people, their lives, problems, sentiments and aspirations. Politics for him was not a matter of high level debate among erudite politicians, it was a matter of selfless service in defence of people's interests..."[58]

Although Gandhi's arrival in India had been accompanied by his experience as well as fame of a long and successful political struggle in South Africa, he chose to abide by Gokhale's advice to rediscover India for himself, before embarking on his own 'experiments'. The process of rediscovering India was revealing, painful and appalling, exposing beyond doubt, the irreparable harm, the colonial regime had done to the country. Confronted with the stark reality of poverty, he soon shed his middle class attire. And this was an express message to the 'dispossessed' that here was a leader who was one of them. It has been argued that Gandhi always denied choosing his "clothes for public relations purposes, their value from this point of view was, however, incontestable."[59] Whether or not Gandhi perceived the change of his attire and adoption of the loincloth as a conscious 'public relations strategy', the change went straight to the millions. In fact, it was a personification of the very image of *Daridranarayan* (the saviour of the poor), the supreme symbol of veneration in Indian culture.

This, indeed, was the essential Gandhi who could 'belittle' neither the 'ethical' nor the 'political' and sought to uncover and to endeavour towards resolving dilemmas of transitional India. To begin with the experiments in *karmyoga*, the opportunities offered by the plight of peasants in Champaran and Kheda and of the mill-workers in Ahmedabad, were used as test-cases for the strategy of *satyagraha*. The 'rebel' Gandhi was yet to transform himself into a 'non-cooperator', a revolutionary Gandhi, caught for quite some time in the Hamlet-dilemma of engaging/disengaging from the Empire in a final sense, although one would not miss his radical, anti-imperialist stance, even in his maiden performance, on the occasion of the inauguration of the Banaras Hindu University on February 4, 1916. He was firm in stating: "If I found it necessary for the salvation of India that the English should retire, that they should be driven out, I would not hesitate to declare that they would have to go and I hope I would be prepared to die in defence of that belief."[60]

The Rowlatt Act of 1918, followed by the Jallianwalla Bagh massacre, however, provided the final breaking-point for the 'idealist' Mahatma to be transformed into a crusader of an anti-imperialist mass struggle. This marked the beginning of a series of innovative experiments in creative political praxis on national level through *satyagraha*. B.R. Nanda has significantly recorded that Lord Curzon who had taken a hand in drafting the declaration of 1917, thought it would take India five hundred years to qualify for self-government. In 1906 Dadabhai Naoroji exhorted Indian nationalists not to succumb to pressure in the face of difficulties. "The Irish have been struggling for 800 years" he wrote "and here they are struggling all the same." A few years later, S.P. Sinha, the first Indian member of the Viceroy's Executive Council, estimated that India would become a dominion in three hundred years. The emergence of Gandhi on the political stage in 1919 upset all these calculations of British statesmen and Indian leaders.[61]

India in 1919 was in an explosive situation. Following the atrocious Jallianwalla Bagh massacre, the enamel of the Empire wore off. To his mortification, Gandhi's worst apprehensions about the perfidy of the imperialist rulers stood vindicated. The growing anti-imperialist stance of the Congress, and indeed, of a large section of the educated middle classes, strengthened Gandhi's resolve to embark upon the first major *satyagraha* on the national level. It has been succinctly observed that the political genius of Gandhi lay "firstly in the ultimate recognition of the situation as revolutionary... and secondly, in finding out a method of direct action suited to a disarmed people to meet a revolutionary situation."[62]

Gandhi's clarion call, inaugurating the progressive non-violent non-cooperation (on August 1, 1920) in *Young India* of July 28, 1920, was resolute and clear: "The power that wrests justice from an unwilling government... is the power of *satyagraha*, whether it is known by the name of civil disobedience or non-cooperation..." The commencement was to be 'marked by fasting and prayer', coupled with the suspension of business and by meetings to pass resolutions praying for the revision of peace terms and justice for the Punjab and for inculcating non-cooperation until justice had been done. Gandhi was optimistic and also confident about the efficacy of his proposed symbolist strategy, as evidenced by his letter to Srinivas Shastri: "I do not know any contemporary of mine who has reduced fasting and prayer to an exact science and who has reaped a harvest so abundant as I have." Gandhi wished to "infect the nation" with his experience and "make it resort to fasting and prayer, with intelligence, honesty and intensity."[63]

Soon, the nation was truly 'infected' with Gandhi's missionary resolve. The protest, which began with apparently innocuous symbols such as fasting and prayer and *hartal*, spread like wild fire to every nook and corner of the country. Never before was the country so intensely enthralled, awakened and united, determined and resolved, as during the eventful months of 1920-22. People became "the subjects and not the objects of history", as aptly described by Bipan Chandra.[64] Gandhi himself became the most powerful symbol of resurgent Indian nationalism, aspiring for nothing less than *swaraj*.

Swaraj was equated with *swadeshi* and enjoined as the supreme duty (as *swadharma*) of every individual and collectivized in political praxis as *karmyoga* in the form of *satyagraha*. In the process, *charkha* and *khadi* became icons of national self-respect and self-reliance and boycott, a symbol of non-attachment and dignity. The symbol of 'bonfire' (*Holi*) acquired special political significance. The symbol signified the sacred *yajna* of national liberation in its broadest sense. In specific terms, the symbol was employed by Gandhi to accomplish the twin objectives of 'complete non-attachment to possessions' (especially the foreign finery) and 'assertion of national identity'. The underlying objective was to challenge the myth of natural/political/civilizational superiority of the colonizers. People in both urban and rural India responded in large numbers to the agenda of five-fold boycott as well as the broader framework of the constructive programme, as anticipated by Gandhi.

Gandhi's transparent sincerity and all-embracing 'love' as true non-violence, his cultivated bearing and forthright demeanour generated spontaneous trust. It looked as if the masses had finally found a saviour and a mentor. His control of the senses gave 'power' to his word and made his 'controlled thought self-acting', in the most efficacious manner. His complete selflessness and pursuit of *aparigraha* in a true sense, placed him against self-seeking opportunism and crass materialism. He was accepted as the living bastion of profound concern for the lowliest. His amazing grasp of the basic moral premises as well as the objective political dimensions of the colonial rule and a relentless resolve to combat the same capacitated him not only as a paternal figure and a popular leader but also a matchless 'general' and an astute strategist, with a novel method of political redress.

Gandhi was aware that *satyagraha* as corporate action involved complicated questions of leadership, organization, discipline, training and strategy on the one hand and 'spontaneous', 'self-activity' of the masses, on the other. Gandhi was also aware that non-violent and truthful behaviour was much more difficult in collective than in individual *satyagraha*. Yet at the same time he was convinced that anything that millions could do together became charged with a unique power.[65] Nevertheless, an expression of the genius of the people was possible only through a creative 'directing centre' to use Antonio Gramsci's apt expression, capable of anticipating the mass-mind and moulding "what was already there" according to the requirements of the situation. Gandhi's meticulous care in gauging the extent of the people's consciousness and readiness for the struggle aided him in accomplishing the difficult task of integrating, the 'spontaneous self-activity' of the masses and 'conscious direction', in accordance with the precepts of *satyagraha*.[66] Gandhi, it needs to be reiterated, emphasized time and again, that *satyagraha* was not an easy option. It was "to be employed only when anything, except violence and war, is more desirable than the existing state of affairs."[67]

The nation-wide mass movement required an enduring nation-wide organization and the financial resources. The transformation of the Indian National Congress from an urban middle-class based organization into a broad-based network was, therefore, contemplated and also, to a large extent, brought about by Gandhi. It was to be an effective instrument of *satyagraha* at the national level, though Gandhi's political space was in many ways broader than that of the Congress. Besides several structural changes, Gandhi also proposed changes in the style of functioning of the Congress and, indeed, in its very ideological and socio-political priorities. A strong executive machinery and extensive provincial network reaching down to the village-level, use of vernacular languages and of *khadi*, and a radicalization of both the content and the strategy of the anti-imperialist struggle were some of the notable elements of Gandhi's agenda of effective intervention in the style of functioning of the Congress. True, the Congress continued to persist with prefixes such as peaceful, instead of 'non-violent', and legitimate instead of 'truthful'. However, 1919 onwards, non-violence was accepted as a 'policy' (though not as a 'creed') for the limited purpose of winning independence. In many ways, the Congress differed and lagged behind Gandhi's ideals throughout the Freedom Struggle. A pragmatic politician and a democrat as he was, Gandhi seldom insisted beyond a point and usually accepted well-informed criticism and dissent as, what he called, the "ozone of public life".[68]

The nation-wide mass movement also required enormous funds. It is astonishing that notwithstanding his asceticism, Gandhi's financial capabilities were marvellous, as borne out by his successful mobilization of big business houses to contribute enormous amount of funds to the nationalist cause in India (as earlier in South Africa). In ideological terms, however, the same marvellous capability generated suspicion especially among left circles about the 'radical' content of his vision as well as his alternative strategy.[69]

Gandhi was clear, as Tilak before him, that *swaraj* could never be a gift from an alien power. It was a 'birth right', but in the given colonial situation, it had to be fought for, with utmost sincerity, commitment, non-violence, sacrifice and suffering. *satyagraha* was the only viable strategy in his view. As early as 1916, Gandhi declared: 'Look at the history of the British Empire and the British Nation, freedom-loving as it is, it will not be a party to give freedom to a people who will not take it themselves'.[70] Similarly, in an open letter "To Every Englishman in India" (*Young India*, 27 October, 1920) Gandhi expounded: "I know you would not mind if we could fight and wrest the sceptre from your hands... we are powerless to do that for you have ensured our incapacity to fight in open and honourable battle. Bravery on the battlefield is thus impossible for us. Bravery of the soul still remains open to us... I am engaged in evoking that bravery. Non-cooperation means nothing less than training in self-sacrifice."[71] Gandhi's call was characterized by a sense of urgency—reverberating all—the leaders, the cadres, the masses. *Karmyoga* became the call of the day, as Gandhi envisioned it.

True, in 1920, Gandhi wanted *swaraj* in an year. He failed, *swaraj* was nowhere in sight, yet the heightened spirit of the people was unprecedented. They forgot for the time being their logic and their sense of the actual and the possible and worked as if their lives depended upon the fulfilment of the dream they considered for the time being as reality.[72] People responded to Gandhi's symbolist strategy in a remarkable measure although several analysts point out the limits of the movement and hold that the response varied considerably from one area to another. In a telegram to the Secretary of State, sent on February 9, 1920, the Viceroy stated: "The lower classes in the town have been seriously affected by the non-cooperation movement... And although (its) influence... has been much smaller in the rural tracts generally, in certain areas the peasantry have been affected, particularly in parts of the Assam Valley, United Provinces, Bihar and Orissa and Bengal. The Government of India are prepared for disorder of a more formidable nature than has in the past occured, and do not seek to minimize in anyway the fact that great anxiety is caused by the situation."[73] Thus, in terms of the nationalist movement, the situation was transformed for ever. Political life in India was never to be the same again. Despite ostensible failure, the Non-Cooperation Movement, could not be termed as a failure. It was one of the facets of the long-term strategy of *satyagraha*, in broad theoretical terms. In terms of political praxis, it was the first major experiment in mass mobilization on non-violent lines.

Notwithstanding the ensuing debates between the non-cooperators and the *swarajists* (1924-26) and later between the adherents of dominion status and complete independence (1928-29), Gandhi was granted full powers to decide the course of the struggle for complete independence, at the Lahore session of the Congress in 1929.

In 1930, Gandhi came out with what Judith Brown has termed 'a superbly ingenious choice', namely, the symbol of salt. The ceremonial civil breach of salt law was accomplished on April 6, 1930. The choice of 'salt' again symbolized Gandhi's identification with "the poorest among the poor who got a bit of food even after starving for two days had to pay his share of the tax on every morsel that he ate..." Salt meant sustenance. Gandhi argued that he was pointing out what was obvious, but it was not being seriously realized. No evidence was needed to prove that more salt was consumed by the poor than the rich for the simple reason that strenuous physical activity resulting in profuse perspiration was undertaken by the former. Therefore, in Gandhi's view, the salt tax was a blatant violation of the very basic norms of civilized life. For an average peasant in India the annual tax was equivalent to his three days' income.[74]

Contrary to skepticism in various quarters, Gandhi was optimistic about the revolutionary possibilities inherent in his call to defy the salt law. He himself described it as "a call of his inner voice". The Governor General and his bureaucracy contemptuously dismissed it as a 'crazy scheme', and a fancy to upset the mighty empire with a 'pinch of salt'. Even the Congress leaders were at a loss to comprehend the potential of a minor symbol like 'salt' in generating and sparking off a revolutionary movement, particularly at places which were away from the sea-coast, where people got their salt by purchasing it from the traders.[75] Here, as Erikson has aptly commented: "Gandhi's shrewdness seemed to join his capacity to focus on the infinite meaning in finite things..."[76]

And before the government and the sceptics could realize the power of Gandhi's call, salt became a symbol of *swaraj*. Dandi March (240 mile walk from Sabarmati to Dandi) emerged as a pilgrimage of protest. The Civil Disobedience Movement did not stop with Dandi. It was perceptibly extended to civil breach of ordinances, no-tax campaigns, defiance of press laws, the boycott agenda of Non-Cooperation Movement. Of all the instances of civil disobedience undertaken during 1930-34, the raids on the salt works at Dharsana exposed to the world at large, the fangs and claws of the Imperial Government in all its ugliness and ferocity, as "the most devilish, cold-blooded and unjustified in the history of nations". Yet the surprising feature was the discipline of the volunteers... thoroughly imbued with Gandhi's non-violent creed, as reported in a moving account by the United Press American Correspondent, Webb Miller in the *New Freeman*.[77] The movement might not have accomplished immediate concrete gains, it certainly marked a distinct moral victory, a renewed zeal and national self-confidence among the common people---not only men but also women---a real break-through in Indian public life. The movement, in terms of its political impact, was phenomenal, with new dimensions of *satyagraha* evolving in the process.

Prologned confrontation leading to the eventual agreement with the Viceroy (Gandhi-Irwin Pact), gave rise to misgivings about Gandhi's mode of political functioning.[78] However, Gandhi himself explained the significance of the admissibility, in *satyagraha*, of reasonableness and responsiveness to opportunities of dialogue. Gandhi-Irwin Pact as well as Gandhi's decision to attend the Second Round Table Conference---apart from the pragmatic political logic---could also be understood in terms of the conceptual reasoning of *satyagraha*, as what Anatol Rappoport calls "transcendence of dichotomy". Because, ultimately as V.V. Ramana Murti has insightfully explained, the "way of violence works as a monologue" but "the nature of non-violence is a dialogue."[79] The aforementioned political steps, then, may be seen as attempts at penetrating the walls of prejudices of the adversary, on the part of the *satyagrahi* Gandhi.

The empire's moral facade was further exposed through the Communal Award (August 17, 1932). Gandhi protested against the Award through 'a perpetual fast unto death'. The fast was dubbed by the British as a thinly disguised coercive strategy with a specific political motive. It was also said that the fast was a diversion, probably aimed at recovering the prestige lost in the decline of the civil disobedience.[80] The symbolist dimensions of Gandhi's technique of 'fasting' were dismissed, even misinterpreted by the pragmatic, wily imperialists. The reverse was not expected. However, the message of the fast went straight to those who mattered. Public opinion was aroused on the issue as never before. The issue dramatized through the fast became a life-long mission for Gandhi, as another form of *satyagraha*, viz., a struggle for Social Swaraj through the constructive programme.

As for the empire, it sought to regain moral initiative once again through constitutional reforms. The result was the Government of India Act of 1935. Gandhi initially supported the scheme to be soon disillusioned and disgusted. And, paradoxical as it may sound, by 1939 when the forces of violence were overshadowing the entire world, Gandhi reasserted his faith in the efficacy of non-violence, although the Congress preferred to deal with the question of 'war' in relation to India's self-government, rather than the creed of non-violence. The Congress, especially the left-wing radicals, wanted Gandhi to launch a mass Civil Disobedience Movement against the imperial regime and its calculated policies denying any assurance of freedom for India in the near future. Instead, judging the time as inopportune for a mass movement, Gandhi started individual *satyagraha* (October 17, 1940) followed by what he called 'representative *satyagraha*', with a view to averting "public excitement and harassment of the authorities" during the war. The 'symbolic' *satyagraha* continued till May 1941. It was not considered 'right' by Gandhi to convert the individual and the representative *satyagraha* into a mass movement, as it could betray the spirit of *satyagraha* itself.

Following the failure of the Cripps Mission, the Congress

'high-command' approached Gandhi once again (January 1942) requesting him to assume leadership. Gandhi's response was unanticipated: it was the 'Quit India' resolution. It has been rightly commented that 'Quit India' was "Gandhi's solution for the two perils of Japanese invasion and internal disunity which confronted India in the summer of 1942."[81] However, Gandhi was largely misunderstood. The 'Quit India' proposals raised the political temperature in the country once again. The government overreacted and the top leaders of the Congress were arrested in the early hours of August 9, 1942. The following events witnessed unparalleled mass consciousness and action. True, there was sporadic violence, but it was largely the consequence of the imperial policies of internment of the top leadership and thereby closing possibilities of any proper direction to the protesters to combat repression. The logic of the events was rather obvious: Gandhi had no right to expect the government to play the game according to his rules, but the government equally had no right to blame him for the consequences of the policy it adopted.[82]

In terms of the precepts of *satyagraha*, the events of 1942 could be deciphered as an embarrassing legacy, as aberration of the creed of non-violence. However, if judged on the anvil of political praxis in the given situation (of a leader-less political scenario and the imperialist repression), the 1942 experience also unfolded a self-generated, 'self-acting' momentum, for which Gandhi had been working hard for two decades. It could also be that the urge for freedom transcended the borders of cautious politics and criss-crossed violence *en route*. Besides, the nature of violence was sporadic and unplanned and not 'premeditated' as alleged by the government. It was, therefore, absolutely misplaced to saddle Gandhi with any kind of responsibility for the outbreak of violence. Gandhi's own response was his twenty-one day fast, notably the only fast against a Viceroy.

With Gandhi and the Congress away from the political scene, Jinnah and the Muslim League got the political space for aggressive communalism. Consequently, by the time Gandhi was released from gaol in 1944, India had been overtaken by the divisive theo-political manoeuvres, reversing all that Gandhi had stood and fought for, throughout his life. Ironically, the symbols Gandhi had employed for national resurrection—political and social—were used to thwart, indeed, sabotage his dream. And, in the face of widespread communal delinquency, Gandhi's last fast (13-17 January, 1948) assuaged the injured humanity of India, though it could not have undone the political disintegration of the country. Gandhi himself viewed the question of the validity of non-violence and *satyagraha* as independent of his own success or failure.

Regarding the efficacy of non-violent *satyagraha*, it has, often, been suggested that Gandhi was fortunate in being pitted against a relatively 'liberal political system' and a 'civilized adversary'.[83] Telling evidence of imperial repression, however, point toward a contrary conclusion. It has been rightly pointed out that the British were careful not to repeat the Amritsar massacre of 1919 but when it came to repressing 'sedition' as they described it, they were not held back by any 'misplaced' humanity. The timing and the quantum of force used against the *satyagraha* struggles were intended to ensure the most favourable results from the official point of view.[84] Indeed, Gandhi's insistence on discriminating protest against imperialist 'measures and systems' and not against men, complicated the matters further for the imperial regime. It was a unique case of moral rectitude in political arena.

It was part of Gandhi's genius that he was able to integrate in his political praxis, a realistic appraisal of power relations between the colonial regime and the colonized, mass support for his strategy and also a subtle and effective appeal to the humane-democratic people in Britain and elsewhere. *Satyagraha*, as a technique, was conceived not only to broaden and intensify protest against the British rule but also to free those already committed to such protest from the 'fears' that had paralyzed them, earlier. *Satyagraha* involved a series of incessant 'experiments with truth', to use Gandhi's favourite refrain, accepting protest against a *duragrahi* (untruthful) regime, as a moral imperative. The moral imperative obviated the need for humiliating confrontation for either of the protagonists and called for voluntary self-suffering as a potential political weapon, variantly interpreted as a strategy of coercion and conversion,[85] cutting through "the rationalized defences of the opponent."[86]

The moral core, the most significant aspect of *satyagraha*, linked the political and the human dimensions of the strategy. The reasons for being moral were intrinsic to human existence itself, in Gandhi's view. Therefore, to be human was to be moral and also to be "one's own self" (at individual, national even global levels). This was *swaraj*, in a true sense, and *satyagraha* was the appropriate strategy to attain it, in any situation of conflict or crisis.

Thus, Gandhian *satyagraha* was simultaneously an innovative/efficacious 'symbolist' strategy, successfully employed for collective political action and a trans-political mode of transformation. As borne out by the preceding discussion, the unprecedented appeal of Gandhi and his *satyagraha* technique is explicable in terms of the rich Indian heritage of symbols to which Gandhi referred time and again, the specific political content that he imparted to numerous ostensible religio-cultural symbols and the new secular political symbols that he created in the process. The idiom of symbols proved immensely useful in getting Gandhi's strategy easily comprehended, readily trusted and actively supported by the common people. During the long freedom struggle, *satyagraha* might have stopped short of people's involvement and participation on a large scale, but for its strong symbolist content and mode of communication, on the part of the creative, imaginative Gandhi. The symbolist content provided valuable authenticity to the political strategy of *satyagraha* in the given historical context, without, notably, weakening its theoretical and universalist transformative potential in disparate contexts, indeed, turning *satyagrahi* Gandhi himself into the most powerful symbol of protest and revolution.

Notes

1. *CWMG*, Vol. XV, p. 312.
2. See 'Satyagraha: Its significance', *Satyagraha* Leaflet Series No. 6, included in Raghavan Iyer (ed.) *The Moral and Political Writings of Mahatma Gandhi*, Vol. III Oxford, Clarendon, 1987, pp. 55-57.
3. M.K. Gandhi, *From Yervada Mandir*, Ahmedabad, Navajivan, 1957, pp. 1-2.
4. Chandra Shankar Shukla, *Conversations of Gandhiji*, Bombay, Vora & Co., 1949, p. 35.
5. Bal Gangadhar Tilak, *Gita Rahasya or The Science of Karmyoga*, (2 volumes), Poona, Tilak Brothers, 1936, p. 964.
6. *CWMG*, LXIX, p. 33.
7. *An Autobiography*, Ahmedabad, Navajivan, 1966, p. 382.
8. See, for instance, Tilak's letter to Gandhi dated 18th January, 1920 and Gandhi's reply dated 28th January, 1920. Reproduced in D.K. Gosavi, *Tilak, Gandhi and Gita*, Bombay, Bhartiya Vidya Bhavan, 1983, pp. 51-52.
9. Mahadev Desai (ed.), *The Gospel of Selfless Action or the Gita According to Gandhi*, Ahmedabad, Navajivan, 1956. See chapters 3 & 4.
10. *Note 7*, p. 71 & 131.
11. S. Radhakrishnan, *The Bhagwad Gita*, London, George Allen & Unwin, 1970, p. 135.

12. *Note 7*, p. 132.
13. C. Rajagopalachari, *Gandhiji's Teachings and Philosophy*, Bombay, Bhartiya Vidya Bhavan, 1963, p. 16. It is notable that Rajaji even went to the extent of saying: "What Gandhiji taught was nothing more or less than what was contained in *The Gita*".
14. *Note 7*, p. 208.
15. *Young India*, December 20, 1928, p. 420.
16. *Note 3*, pp. 45-48.
17. *Note 16*.
18. *Speeches and Writings of Mahatma Gandhi*, Madras, Natesan, 1922, p. 494.
19. Joan V. Bondurant, *Conquest of Violence: The Gandhian Philosophy of Conflict* (Rev. ed.) Berkeley, University of California Press, 1967, pp. 20-21.
20. *Harijan*, March 2, 1940, p. 23.
21. *Harijan*, January 7, 1939, p. 417.
22. *Harijan*, May 6, 1939, p. 113. Also see, *Harijan*, March 14, 1936, p. 39.
23. *Harijan*, March 23, 1940, p. 55.
24. *Young India*, December 31, 1931, pp. 427-28.
25. Jawaharlal Nehru, *An Autobiography*, Bombay, Allied, 1962, pp. 505-506.
26. For details refer to V.G. Panov, *Emotions, Myths and Theories*, Moscow, Progress, 1985, pp. 23-24.
27. G. Bergmann, *The Metaphysics of Logical Positivism*, London, Longman, Green & Co., 1954, p. 45. Quoted in *Note* 26.
28. *Note 26*, pp. 137-163.
29. S. Radhakrishnan, *An Idealist View of Life*, London, Unwin Books, 1961, p. 149.
30. *Note 29*, pp. 152-153.
31. Chandrashankar Shukla, *Gandhi's View of Life*, Bombay, Bhartiya Vidya Bhavan, 1951, pp. 36-37. Interestingly, Shukla cites five instances of national importance when Gandhi acted on the call of his 'inner voice' during 1926-34.
32. *Young India*, December 31, 1931, pp. 427-428.

33. H.S. Polak, H.N. Brailsford and Lord Pethick Lawrence, *Mahatma Gandhi*, London, Odhams Press, 1949 p. 210. Quoted in *Note 30*, p. 40.
34. Raghavan N. Iyer, *The Moral and Political Thought of Mahatma Gandhi*, Delhi, Oxford University Press, 1973, pp. 122-123.
35. See, *Indian Opinion*, October 8, 1931.
36. See, M.K. Gandhi, *Satyagraha in South Africa* (1928), Ahmedabad, Navajivan, 1993.
37. *Harijan*, March 28, 1936, p. 49.
38. *Harijan*, September 5, 1936, p. 49.
39. M.K. Gandhi, *Non-violence in Peace and War*, Vol. I (1942), Ahmedabad, Navajivan, 1962, p. 416.
40. *Note 39*, p. 396.
41. *Harijan*, July 27, 1947, p. 253.
42. *Note 3*, p. 14.
43. *Harijan*, May 30, 1938, p. 125.
44. See, for instance, Erik Erikson, *Gandhi's Truth*, New York, W.W. Norton & Co., 1969, pp. 400-409.
45. *Harijan*, November 21, 1936, p. 321.
46. *Note 3*, pp. 19-22.
47. *Note 3*, pp. 23-26.
48. *Note 47*.
49. *Note 3*, p. 93, Also *Harijan*, June 1, 1939, p. 125.
50. Note 3, p. 43.
51. S.H. Rudolph and L.I. Rudolph, *Gandhi: The Traditional Roots of Charisma*, Hyderabad, Orient Longman, 1987, p. 40.
52. B.R. Nanda, *Gandhi and His Critics*, Delhi, Oxford Paperbacks, 1993, p. 67.
53. Hiren Mukherjee, *Gandhiji: A Study*, New Delhi, People's Publishing House, 1979 (3rd ed.) pp. 192-193.
54. See M.K. Gandhi, *Hind Swaraj* (1909), Ahmedabad, Navajivan, 1938.
55. J.B. Kripalani, *Gandhi: The Statesman*, Delhi, Ranjit Publishers, 1951, pp. 21-22.

56. *Note 51*, p. 77.
57. *Note 53*, p. 40.
58. E.M.S. Namboodiripad, *The Mahatma and the Ism*, Bombay, People's Publishing House, 1959, p. 19.
59. See for instance, Geoffrey Ashe, *Gandhi: A Study in Revolution*, Calcutta, Asia, 1968, p. 148.
60. *The Selected Works of Mahatma Gandhi* (Henceforth cited as *SW*) Shriman Narayan (ed.), Ahmedabad, Navajivan, 1968, Vol. VI, p. 11.
61. *Note 52*, p. 57.
62. *Note 55*, p. 19.
63. See Gandhi's letter to Srinivas Shastri, *SW*, Vol. V, pp. 69-70.
64. Bipan Chandra, *Essays on Indian Nationalism*, New Delhi, Har-Anand, 1993, p. 11.
65. *Harijan*, April 7, 1946, p. 72.
66. *Note 64*, pp. 80-85.
67. K. Shridharani, *War Without Violence*, Bombay, Bhartiya Vidya Bhavan, 1962, p. 274.
68. *Harijan*, November 13, 1937, p. 33.
69. This is a debatable point. See, for instance, Bipan Chandra, *Note 64*, who argues out a case for the pro-nationalist instance of the Indian Industrialists. Also see B.R. Nanda, *Note 52* for a contrary viewpoint.
70. *SW*, Vol. VI, p. 14.
71. *SW*, Vol. III, pp. 100-101.
72. *Note 55*, pp. 88-89.
73. Quoted in Michael Brecher, *Nehru: A Political Biography*, London, Oxford University Press, 1959, pp. 78-79.
74. See Gandhi's Letter to Lord Irwin, *SW*, Vol. V, pp. 191-196.
75. Rajendra Prasad, *At the Feet of Mahatma Gandhi*, Calcutta, Asia, 1961, pp. 168-169.
76. Eric H. Erikson, *Life History and the Historical Moment*, New York, W.W. Norton & Co., 1975, p. 156.

    Also see pp. 155-160, for a useful discussion of Ernest Jones' interpretation of the symbolic significance of salt as human semen and Victor Wolfenstein's diagnosis of Gandhi's choice of salt-tax as the issue of political movement.

77. B.R. Nanda, *Mahatma Gandhi* (1958) Delhi, Oxford India Paperbacks, 1989, pp. 167-168.
78. See for details, Judith M. Brown, *Gandhi and Civil Disobedience: The Mahatma in Indian Politics-1928-34*, CUP, 1977, pp. 155-168.
79. See V.V. Ramana Murti, "Buber's Dialogue and Gandhi's Satyagraha", *The Journal of the History of Ideas*, 29, 1968, p. 608 (pp. 605-613).
80. See *Note 78*, pp. 318-323.
81. *Note 77*, p. 229.
82. *Note 77*, p. 233.
83. See for instance, George Orwell, *The Collected Essays, Journalism and Letters of George Orwell*, Vol. IV, Harmondsworth, Penguin, 1970, p. 329.

    Also See, J. Bandyopadhyaya, *Social and Political Thought of Gandhi*, Bombay, Allied, 1969, p. 343.
84. *Note 52*, p. 63.
85. See for instance, Thomas Weber, *Conflict Resolution and Gandhian Ethics*, New Delhi, The Gandhi Peace Foundation, 1991; Chapter 2, Also See R.B. Gregg, *The Power of Non-violence*, Ahmedabad, Navajivan, 1960.
86. *Note 19*, p. 228.

5

Symbols of Social Reconstruction

Renovation, Inversion, Innovation

> "I am not interested in freeing India merely from the English yoke. I am bent upon freeing India from any yoke whatsoever. I have no desire to exchange 'king log' for 'king stork'."[1]

Gandhi's conception of the "construction of *Purna Swaraj* by truth and non-violent means" entailed a comprehensive constructive programme.[2] The programme comprised an elaborate, careful deliberation of duties, conceptualized as *Swadharma* and communicated to the masses in terms of various symbols. It was a distinctive Gandhian strategy of social reconstruction, rejecting and transcending the modern liberal view of self as a "disengaged self" (Taylor) or an "unencumbered subject" (Sandel) on the one hand, and the logic of binary oppositions and confrontationist postures on the other. As central to the entire vision and struggle for *swaraj*, Gandhi visualized a total reconstruction of Indian society from bottom upwards, characterized by the democratic values of equality, empathy and mutual respect between sexes, castes and communities. *Swaraj*, in his view, was impossible if the social order was corrupt.[3] Social reconstruction, therefore, required a radical restructuring not only of basic social institutions of Indian society but also of norms and attitudes, at both individual and collective levels.

Gandhi attempted to do this by reinterpreting and selectively using tradition, in a 'post-traditional' manner for the long-term objective of *Purna Swaraj*. In the process, Gandhi renovated some aspects of Indian tradition, inverted others and also undertook some innovative experiments. Though Gandhi predominantly remained a traditionalist, he was not a conventionalist. On the contrary, he was a radical, "highly subversive of the mainstream of Indian, particularly, Hindu culture" as Ashis Nandy argues.[4] His re-reading of Indian culture and tradition was "extremely creative". By attributing all his statements to the roots in the Indian civilization and particularly Hinduism, he created a picture of Hinduism which made it possible for its followers to accept modern values.[5] His objective, in an ultimate sense, was regeneration of Indian society, compatible with his ideal of *Purna Swaraj*, that is, of an 'egalitarian-communitarian' society, as discussed earlier in this study.

Gandhi's strategy of social reconstruction is distinctively marked by his revolt against, and change in some of the core aspects of India's social structure, rooted in Hindu tradition, though he proudly proclaimed that his desire to 'purify' Hinduism was ascribable to his faith in Hindu (*Sanatan*) *dharma*, in its original, Vedic version. The seeming paradox, of what he proclaimed and what he did, is possible to resolve if his agenda for social transformation is seen as integral to his strategy and vision of *swaraj*. Far from confusing uncertainty or ambivalence, Gandhi could ascertain that it was "good to swim in the waters of tradition, but to sink in them is suicide."[6] Critiquing one's own roots, where necessary, was as much an act of *swaraj* as questioning the alien *raj*, and the alien civilization. Gandhi, then, was both a 'traditionalist' and a 'radical'. He was, in this sense, a "rooted radical", markedly different from his predecessors—the nineteenth century reformers and early twentieth century liberals and the militants—and also from his contemporaries, particularly, the left-radicals. Without any pretentious big labels he clearly specified "the spinning wheel, Hindu-Muslim unity and removal of untouchability" as the keys to *swaraj*.[7]

Swadeshi was the most significant strategy. It was a far-sighted strategy "to unite the national movement with economic struggles" as Irfan Habib has rightly observed.[8] In terms of vision, *swadeshi* was as architectonic as *swaraj*. It was advocated by Gandhi as the supreme duty of every Indian to counter the imperialist exploitative, politico-economic and cultural hegemony. It is important to note that *swadeshi* was explained not merely as a countering design but as an exemplification of *swadharma*—a pious duty of every Indian. In practical terms, it was brought home to people through highly innovative and ingenious symbols, viz., *charkha* (the spinning wheel) and *khadi*. Beneath these exogenous symbols lay the instrumental symbolism of ideals like *asteya*, *aparigraha* and bread labour. *Swadeshi* also stood for consolidation of cottage industries and emancipation of rural India, alternative indigenous educational scheme, conceived as a corrective to the imposed western education, and propagation of *Rashtrabhasha*, organization of peasants, labour force and students, efforts for economic equality, and education in hygiene, health and nature cure. *Swadeshi* could, thus, be seen as a powerful ideology of socio-econo-cultural transformation, conducive to and running parallel to the political struggle. It was truly synonymous with *swaraj*.

Swadharma was reinterpreted and expanded to include *sambhava* as a duty, a social obligation in specific terms of removal of untouchability at one level, and removal of communal tensions, at another. The question of women's rights and gender equality also formed a vital part of Gandhi's agenda of social transformation. Constructive programme for social regeneration was, thus, conceived and presented through an expansive range of symbols, at once individual and collective, specific and general, endogenous and exogenous. Gandhi's symbolism at times, appears, exceptionally daring, in his deep concern and commitment to socio-economic reconstruction.

Deriving the central tenet of "mandate for action" that is *karma*, from his perennial reference book, the *Bhagwad Gita*, and defining action as "a moral as well as a physical necessity,"[9] as *yajna*, as performance of duty, as *swadharma*, and as "body labour for service,"[10] Gandhi imaginatively extended the same to the public realm. As discussed earlier, he insisted that *swaraj* for a people meant the sum total of the *swaraj* (self-rule) of all the individuals. And *swaraj* of the above order could be attained only by performance of duty by each citizen.[11] Gandhi also stressed that people who obtain rights as a result of performance of duty, exercise them only for the service of society, never for themselves.[12] *Swadharma*, therefore, became the central referent for the architectonic symbol of *swaraj*, for *satyagraha*, for constructive programme, and for *swadeshi* and *samabhava*.

Like other essential aspects of his philosophy, constructive programme comprised both a vision for the future as well as an 'action-strategy' for the given situation. The strategy was notably historically situated as it was a response to the challenges of the frustrating ethos of an economy, thriving on exploitation and a social structure inhibited by sterile practices.

Though a systematized statement of the constructive programme was published by Gandhi in 1941, and modified in 1945,[13] it had always been a part and parcel of his *satyagraha* movement, beginning with his experiments in South Africa.[14] In India, it could be seen as preceding the formal *satyagraha* movements, evident in the Sabarmati Ashram activities and Ashram-sponsored activities during 1915-1919. Hereafter it was pursued, as G.N. Dhawan rightly remarks, as the means of generating moral strength, preceding non-violent direct action, as a means of consolidation and as an antidote to any possible intoxication of a victory or depression of a set-back.[15] Though at times Gandhi did not insist upon pursuance of the constructive programme as imperative for local civil disobedience, for instance, in the case of Bardoli. But even in the case of Bardoli as Richard Gregg points out, Gandhi attributed much of the success to the fact that a constructive economic and social programme of reform had been going on there for six or seven years prior to that.[16] Thus, constructive programme was closely intertwined with *satyagraha*, in Gandhian thought and praxis.

The basic concern for bread for the masses and honourable means to get it, that is, the fundamental right to survival with dignity, led Gandhi to conceptualize *swadeshi* as the foundation of *swaraj*. The edifice of *swaraj*, "built up brick by brick by corporate self-effort" would be in peril if not supported by the solid pillars of social justice and harmony. The significance of social justice and communal amity was ably conveyed by Gandhi through the moral precept of *samabhava*. For Gandhi, *swadeshi* as an extension of *swadharma* was as "consistent with the law of humility and love", as with true ethical core of economics.[17]

The powerful symbolism of *swadeshi* was vivified through *charkha* and *khadi* that became synonymous with the urges, aspirations and identity of resurgent India, 'electrifying' the entire atmosphere, as Gandhi had anticipated.[18] At one level, *charkha* and *khadi* were equated with "the supremacy of man in place of supremacy of power-driven machine over him,"[19] at another, "as a religious and economic necessity... fraught with political consequences of a lofty moral ideal in order that all may take part in it..." It is the 'human element' on which the entire economics of *khadi* rests,[20] because to a people famished and forced into idleness, the only acceptable form in which God can dare appear is work and promise of food as wages.[21] *Khadi* was conceived as "the beginning of economic freedom and equality of all in the country" as a "wholesale *swadeshi* mentality, a determination to find all the necessaries of life in India and that too through the labour and intellect of the villagers", ensuring total decentralization of the production and distribution of the most vital essentialities of life.[22]

Gandhi was convinced that only the revival of hand-spinning and hand-weaving could ensure the economic and moral regeneration of India. The millions needed "a simple industry to supplement agriculture". Postulating historical authenticity of his contention, Gandhi maintained that "spinning was the cottage industry years ago, and if millions are to be saved from starvation, they must be enabled to reintroduce spinning in their homes."[23] In Gandhi's view, spinning was the fittest sacrificial body labour, not less than worship of God: "I cannot imagine anything nobler or more national than that, for say one hour in a day. We should all do the labour that the poor must do, and thus identify ourselves with them and through them with all the mankind."[24]

As discussed earlier also, the message of the spinning wheel was 'wider than its circumference'—one of simplicity, service of mankind, living so as not to hurt others, creating an indissoluble bond between the rich and the poor, capital and labour, the prince and the peasant.[25] Gandhi apprehended that the root cause of poverty in India lay in 'want of work' for the common masses. As a staunch advocate of the dignity of labour, akin to Karl Marx, Gandhi unequivocally defended the spinning wheel thus: "Labour is money. He who provides dignified labour for the millions in their cottages, provides food and clothing, or which is the same thing as money. The *charkha* provides such labour."[26] The *charkha* was also identified by Gandhi as a therapeutic device: "Idleness is the great cause, the root of all evil and if that root can be destroyed, most of the evils can be remedied without further effort. A nation that is starving has little hope or initiative left in it... That winter of despair can be turned into the 'sun-shine' of hope for the millions only through the life-giving wheel, the *charkha*."[27]

It is important to bear in mind that in parts of rural India, weavers were treated as untouchables. Weavers of coarse *khadi*, were the worst affected, as machine-made foreign cloth was dumped on an unsuspecting people. As the movement for *swadeshi* gained ground, *khadi* came to their rescue. The masses soon realized that the cloth signified more than a household product. As large numbers of untouchables subsisted on spinning in rural India *charkha* and *khadi* became "doubly the poor man's staff of life". More so, as the untouchables were the most helpless among the poorest, because many occupations, which were available to others were not available to them.[28] The spinning wheel generating 'good will and self-help', symbolized 'commercial peace' in place of 'commercial war'.[29] Gandhi envisioned *charkha* as a harbinger of a silent and sure revolution of non-violent economic self-sufficiency, though he was aware of the numerous impediments. He called upon the "selfless Indians of intelligence and patriotism working with a single mind in the villages to spread the message of the *charkha*... a mighty effort at cooperation and adult education of the correct type."[30]

With the spinning wheel as the nodal point, revival of *khadi* was to be followed by rehabilitation of other village industries, for in Gandhi's view, in the long run, real *swaraj* depended upon the rejuvenation of village-life as a whole. *Khadi*, however, remained the central instrument of redemption and generation of "spontaneous strength for *Swaraj*"[31], symbolizing the "unity of Indian humanity, of its economic freedom and equality and, therefore, ultimately, in the poetic expression of Jawaharlal Nehru, "the livery of India's freedom".[32]

If Gandhi placed *khadi* and *charkha* prior to communal amity and the removal of untouchability, he had a pragmatic reason and a sound logic in mind: "If I wish to work half an hour a day for Hindu-Muslim unity or removal of untouchability I would be hard put to imagine what to do. But the plying of the spinning wheel for an hour is concrete work."[33] The unequivocal faith in the creative potential of purposive activity by the large masses, ostensibly for a national cause, impelled him to declare: "Give me the spinning-wheel and I will spin Swaraj for India."[34]

This is not to suggest that Gandhi undermined other aspects of socio-economic regeneration. As stated earlier, equating *swadeshi* and *swadharma*, he extended his call to related village-industries, and advocated *swavalamban* (self-reliance) and *swabhiman* (dignity of the self). Similarly, *samabhava* emerged in his thought, as the pillar of social justice, aimed specifically, at the removal of untouchability and of gender inequality and for forging communal amity. More specifically, it was conceived to expose and combat 'the satanic' implications of the western, urban, mechanized, industrial civilization.

Missionary commitment to eradication of untouchability was a human and ethical precondition of national unity and social justice, for Gandhi, prompting him to elevate the cause as a 'vow', and demanding strict adherence to it, particularly by the Congress workers. In keeping with his faith in the philosophy of *advaita*, it was an axiomatic call of his *swadharma* (as he interpreted it) "to break down the barriers between man and man and between the various orders of being and to serve all life as one's own self."[35] Castigating untouchability as "a soul destroying sin"[36], Gandhi's unswerving conviction made him declare that he would renounce Hinduism "if it was true that untouchability was a part of Hinduism."[37] Nothing could have been more radical for a man who prided himself on being a true Hindu, for, the actual essence of Hinduism for him, was *advaita*, the philosophy of unity of all life, manifesting the spark of one and the same divine source. Untouchability was absolutely out of place and antithetical to Hinduism in its essential form. It had no scriptural sanction behind it. It was an unfortunate accretion later added by the vested interests. The accretion had done enormous harm to Hinduism and was threatening India's very social fabric.

There could be no justification for condemning individuals and social groups as 'impure' and 'unequal' owing to birth in a particular segment of society, in Gandhi's view. In fact, he had the courage to assail and reject the feudalistic hierarchy of social status as it evolved to pervert the functional efficacy of specialization, based not on birth but on specific identification of one's qualitative potential and manifest proclivity.[38] Instead of floundering his efforts in superficial debate, Gandhi assailed the very root of the evil. Though Gandhi was not skeptical about the pristine purposiveness of the *varna* system he never diluted his contempt for the caste system as an unmitigated "social evil".[39] He argued that if "*varna* reveals the law of one's being and thus the duty one has to perform it confers no right and the idea of superiority or inferiority is wholly repugnant to it. All *varnas* are equal, for the community depends no less on one than on another... gradations of high and low... is hideous travesty of the original."[40] He clarified: "Varnashram is not a vertical division. It is a horizontal one. Hence, there can be no question of untouchability."[41]

Ramashray Roy's interpretation is notable in this regard. In his view, Gandhi believed neither in the renunciation of this world and the transcendence of the sphere of action nor in the priority of the *varna dharma*. He recognized the importance of *varna dharma* but emphasized the necessity of informing it with *sadharana dharma*. However, the ground for commitment to and expression of the common as well as *varna* specific duties does not, in Gandhi's view, lie in either prudential or non-prudential reason. It lies in man's total commitment to the quest for the transcendental centre which constitutes the source not only for man's identity with the external world but also for his morality.[42]

And yet, the societal reality, in all its brazen malignancy is that untouchability has become a part and parcel of the practice of Hinduism. It is, indeed, a plague, which it is the bounden duty of every Hindu to combat.[43] The moral imperative of the removal of untouchability, to Gandhi "means love for and service of the whole world and thus merges into *ahimsa*."[44] Political *swaraj* would be a dead weight in the absence of social justice, obliterating all distinctions of *savarnas* (caste Hindus) and *avarnas* (outcastes). Personal individual endeavour is as important as collective effort to ensure the same.

How could God, the supreme creator, axiomatically above all social distinctions, as *Vishwanath* (Lord of the Universe) permit exclusion of one segment of society from entrance into his presence? The poser had significant symbolist implications. It very clearly brought home the simple truth that barring entry into the temples made the deities of Hinduism non-existent for the untouchables.[45] Gandhi lost no opportunity in advising people to abstain from visits to temples closed to the *Harijans*.[46] Gandhi's ceaseless effort for getting the temples opened for the *Harijans* was neither political expediency nor populism, it was a manifestation of his unrelenting urge for emancipation of the downtrodden and concern for social justice. Following the Travancore Maharaja's Proclamation of temple entry to the *Harijans* in January 1937, Gandhi called upon all high-caste people "to voluntarily become *Harijans* among the *Harijans*, servants of God and let all the world know that all were equal in the eyes of God."[47] The problem was both social and moral for Gandhi. His deep concern agglomerated his faith in 'transformation of heart' (*hridaya parivartan*) on the one hand and change in perspectives through constructive programme on the other. Gandhi rejected any compromise on the issue.

In terms of political praxis, Gandhi's resorting to the traditional Hindu symbolism of fasting and prayer, specifically his 'fast unto death' as a protest against the Communal Award in 1932, needs attention in order to comprehend the multidimensional struggle that Gandhi was engaged in, for the cause of the untouchables. The Communal/MacDonald Award envisaged separate representation to the untouchables partly in response to, and conceding the demands of, B.R. Ambedkar. Gandhi saw it as a fabricated solution, in the form of "separate representation to the minorities". Acceptance of the fabricated solution by Gandhi would have meant complete annihilation of his deep-seated faith in an integral Hindu social order. The untouchables could not be viewed and identified as an exclusive category and segmentalized as a minority. In fact, Gandhi lived their misery, ever since his South African days, voluntarily accepting the life of renunciation. Critics often tend to miss Gandhi's moral and social radicalism on the issue. In a moment of genuine agony he recorded: "I can understand the claims advanced by other minorities, but the claims advanced on behalf of the untouchables is the unkindest out of all. It means the perpetual bar sinister. I would not sell the vital interests of the untouchables for the sake of winning freedom of India... *Will the untouchables remain untouchables in perpetuity?*"[48] (emphasis added).

It is this courage of rectitude that distinguished Gandhi, forever advocating the cause of untouchables as 'equal' to others (Caste Hindus) and as God's chosen ones (*Harijans*). Gandhi was also forthright in his assertion that the untouchables were an 'inseparable' part of the Hindu community. The assertion validated his faith in *ahimsa*, blossoming into compassion, temperance and love.

Gandhi has recently been made the target of unjust affronts on this score, amounting to a sort of confounding of history and suppressing probity of word and action. His 'fast unto death'

(September 20-26, 1932), which was entirely a *satyagrahi's* protest against what he thought was a blatant imperialist ploy to dismember the Hindu social order and a brazen trap to catch one social segment unawares and mislead the other into false expectations of contrived fairplay. Gandhi was not against "even overrepresentation of the depressed classes," but he could not accept "their statutory separation even in a limited form from the Hindu fold, *so long as they choose to belong to it*"[49] (emphasis added). One would not miss Gandhi's abhorrence of any vestige of coercion to force the adversary's reluctance into unwilling compliance. He was, however, firm in his conviction of letting the untouchables exercise their right of self-determination through a referendum after five years of the commencement of the panel system operative through primary and secondary elections, proposed in the Poona Pact. Denis Dalton has rightly commented in this regard: "what is most remarkable is not how much Gandhi himself changed, but indeed, in such a period of history, how he managed to remain in purpose, strength, and method, so fundamentally constant."[50]

What is even more significant is that the 'epic fast' (as Nehru described it) succeeded in bringing untouchability on the national and the Congress agenda as an 'urgent' and a challenging issue. The twenty-one day fast undertaken by Gandhi, immediately following the 'epic fast' symbolized not only Gandhi's earnestness for the cause but also called for greater vigilance and concern. Gandhi did not depend exclusively on the Congress in this regard, and to transform the cause into a crusade, he sought to go beyond the political exertions. He began publication of the *Harijan*, and founded the *Harijan Sevak Sangh*, with a view to extending experiments in socio-psychological engineering through moral self-activating persistence and persuasion. It was a distinctive way of challenging the social hierarchy.

In the larger context of social transformation, the issue of the efficacy of the moral-persuasive approach vis-a-vis the structural-statutory-protectionist approach assumes situational relevance. Strangely, Gandhi endeavoured to consolidate social reciprocity of trust and harmony, even while he was controverting existing values. His sincerity was never in doubt. In fact, with such initial steps, subsequent struggle of the depressed classes assumed added legitimacy. In a glowing tribute, Henry Brailsford characterized Gandhi's campaign against untouchability as "one of the strongest chapters in history and one of the noblest," opening "the road of the untouchables to freedom."[51]

Gandhi was under no illusion of perfect social harmony. He repeatedly insisted that the objective of *swaraj* presupposed as much an external mode of struggle as "reform from within", and could not be achieved without involving all sections of society, howsoever apprehensive about each other's intentions and the imponderables of the outcome.

Accordingly, *swadharma* emerged in Gandhi's vision as catalyst of *Sarva Dharma Sambhava*, specified both as a vow for a *satyagrahi* and a concrete programme of action on the agenda of constructive programme. *Sarva Dharma Sambhava* is also traceable to his spiritual, moral symbolism. Accepting all religions as proceeding from one supreme spirit, that is God, and also converging on the same point, Gandhi's dictum was to "entertain the same respect for the religious faiths of others as we accord to our own."[52] To explain his viewpoint he often used the metaphor of a tree, which has a single trunk but numerous branches and leaves. Likewise, there is a unified core of the true and perfect Religion, which diversifies without negating or undermining the inchoate reality. At the highest spiritual level, the unified core is beyond apprehensive diversions. It is the fallibility of mankind that evolved the varied idioms and expressions manifesting this unified core, leading to a plurality of primacies and interpretations. Religion, in

Gandhi's view, is a source of moral values and may be used for 'reconstructionist' objectives.

Reminiscent of Rousseau, Gandhi muses that everybody is right from his own standpoint, but it is not impossible that everybody is also wrong. Hence, the obligation to nurture a compassionate discernment at individual, social and national levels that called for "our duty to blend into our faith every acceptable feature of other faiths."[53] The concept and practice of *samabhava* is not a negative premise of compulsive or reluctant concession to the pluralistic reality of organized religious sects and systems. It is also not a plea for pseudo-secularism, feigning political neutrality vis-a-vis religious issues. It might be recalled that the notion of political neutrality was the product of confrontation of ecclesiastical and political interests in pre-industrial west. The emphasis in the west was on exclusivity and ostensible separation of religious and political spheres, whereas Gandhi's quest through *sambhava* embodied an inclusivist, humanistic concern for redeeming blurred human sensitivity and conscience not only in matters of faith but also politics. This involved an endeavour for communal amity at one level, and an ontological quest for human salvation in terms of meaningfulness of human existence, at another. The vision of *sambhava* was thus pervasively universalist and inclusivist and broader than secularism in its narrow state-centric political formulation.

Gandhi's insistence on "unprejudiced understanding of world's religions" was, in fact, a sacred duty for him as part of the greater mission of *ahimsa* and truth. He also insisted that true spirituality in contrast to outer piety, was manifest in devotion and service. Accordingly, his prayer meetings included recitations from the *Bhagwad Gita*, and hymns from other principal denominational texts. This was consciously done to inform, articulate and broaden the orientations of people and extend frontiers of understanding and goodwill. This was not a populist strategy but constructive commitment so as "to help a Hindu to become a better Hindu, a Mussalman to become a better Mussalman, and Christian a better Christian."[54] Gandhi was aware that "so long as there are different religions, everyone of them may need some outward distinctive symbol. But when the symbol is made into a fetish and an instrument of proving the superiority of one's religion over others, it is fit only to be discarded."[55] Gandhi was uniquely condescending to have accepted all great religions as fundamentally equal. He was equally firm that only God was absolute and eternal. None of the human formulations of God could be accepted as final or supreme. It was, therefore, an imperative obligation in his view, to inculcate and enliven "not mutual toleration but equal respect"[56] for all systems of faith. This specific emphasis in Gandhi's worldview has often been underplayed by critics, imbalancing his symbolism of *sambhava* in favour of a retrogressive vision.

In Gandhian symbolism, *samabhava* is significant as another dimension of faith in non-violence, which, in his view, far from being confined to the *rishis* (seers) and saints, was practiceable by the common people.[57] In essence, it was "service of the helpless." Thus interpreted; "the spinning wheel, the rosary and the *Ramanama*—all symbolized the same spirit, the religion of service.[58] Gandhi even stated that spinning was superior to the practice of denominational religions. Redefining the *bhakta* (the true devotee) as depicted in the *Gita* as one 'who serves his fellowmen,' Gandhi extended the premise to include conquest of ego and annihilation of the evil within: "And when a man thus loses himself, he immediately finds himself in the service of all that lives."[59] Underlying this is the incontrovertibility of prayer, a call to humility, to self-purification, to inward search, an inveterate spiritual discipline.[60]

Ideally, self-effacing service itself is worship and should need no other symbols. In practice, however, especially for the common man, outer symbols—such as prayer, fasting, *bhajans* (devotional songs/hymns) and the like are conducive props, instrumental in creating the ambience of devotion.[61] The autonomy of the devotee is upheld by Gandhi. The infiniteness of God lies in the fact that he "has a thousand names, or rather He is nameless. We may worship or pray to him by whichever name that pleases us... All worship the same spirit, but as all foods do not agree with all, all names do not appeal to all. Each chooses the name according to his associations..."[62] It is these 'associations' which impart specific subjective meaning to the symbols employed to convey the deeper, underlying ethical core. In Gandhi's comprehension, "whereas the utterance of the word *Rama* will instantaneously affect millions of Hindus, the word 'God', although they may understand the meaning, will leave them untouched." Words after all acquire a power by long usage and sacredness associated with their use.[63] However, he also argued: "My Rama, the Rama of our prayers is not the historical Rama, the son of Dasharatha, the king of Ayodhya. He is the eternal, the unborn, the one without a second... He belongs equally to all. I, therefore, see no reason why a Mussalman or anybody should object to taking his name. But he is in no way bound to recognize God as Rama. He may utter to himself *Allah* or *Khuda* so as not to mar the harmony of the sound.[64] Thus, the magnitude of *samabhava* was intrinsically ethical, inclusivist and secular humanitarian.

The most controversial symbol used by Gandhi was the cow. Gandhi had to explain time and again that his plea for cow-protection was not a denominational advocacy. His concern was for the environmental totality, putting "the animal creation on the same level with man so far as the right to live is concerned." He was insistent that the cow was merely a symbol. For him, he was a poor specimen of Hinduism, who stopped merely at cow protection, when he could extend the arm of protection to other animals. Explaining why the cow-protection was selected for apotheosis, he stated, "the cow was in India the best companion. She was the giver of plenty. Not only did she give milk but she also made agriculture possible... She was the mother to millions of Indian mankind."[65] Advocacy of cow-protection, was in no way obscurantist or sentimental for Gandhi, but an extension of *samabhava*, embracing the human as well as the sub-human creation. Thus interpreted, the cow was more a symbol of an unselfish benefactor and embodiment of mercy and compassion, rather than an exclusive, sacred treasure of Hinduism.

It is significant that when Gandhi talked of Hinduism, it was in ontological rather than rigid scriptural terms. His particular emphasis was on *dharma*, the broadest possible application of 'duty' on one's part, interpreted, specified and meaningfully operationalized as *swadharma* in public life. And more important, *swadharma* as *dharma* could not be conceived without *samabhava*, inclusive of *Sarva Dharma Sambhava*, for in the ultimate analysis *ahimsa*, in its broadest sense, was the highest duty for Gandhi. The ideal of *samabhava* was, thus, an immanent, intrinsic part of the integral philosophy of Gandhi, not something external or imposed or inducted for expediency. It was a prerequisite for both social reconstruction and political independence, in his view.

It is against the conceptual assumptions delineated above that Gandhi's quest for communal amity, during the specific historical expanse of national movement also needs to be evaluated. It calls for an intensive enquiry as to why did Gandhi not succeed in his crusade for national unity, despite a perfect humanistic vision of *Purna Swaraj*. Was it the failure of the vision or of the strategy ? Did the symbolist strategy, so successful on the political front, fall short of the challenging task of communal unity ? Or was it deliberately misrepresented and countered by the vested interests ? It can be plausibly argued that the symbols that Gandhi employed for the purpose were 'purposely misinterpreted' as narrowly 'Hindu', and 'exclusivist' by his adversaries, as part of a calculated strategy to thwart the composite struggle for *swaraj*.

A terse, though misleading observation, sums up the communalist propaganda: "Symbols of Hindu Raj and Hindu culture were adopted in government institutions paid for by all tax payers. Vidya Mandirs, Hindu temples of learning, were opened. Schools began the day by saluting the Congress flag, by singing the 'Bande Matram', a notoriously anti-Muslim song, and by puja, or the worshipping of Gandhi's portrait—a practice deeply obnoxious to Muslims. Insistence on the protection of cows took forms which inflicted economic injury upon the poorer Muslims and enforced submission to sentiments foreign to the Muslim mind."[66]

Clearly, the observation, entirely jaundiced and prejudiced, and in complete disregard of Gandhi's ceaseless efforts for communal understanding, amity and accommodation demonstrates how malafide propaganda was cleverly carried on by the communal separatists, and supported, for their own interests, by the colonial masters.

Even at the risk of digression, it is imperative to look at the whole issue in historical perspective. Right since 1908, Gandhi had been arguing that the seeds of the separatist argument lay in the encounter of India with the colonial power. This encounter resulted in the disintegration of the old order, destroying the prevalent economic infrastructure and autonomous political structures and severely damaging social harmony and the pluralistic universe of India. In the pre-colonial period, differences of religion did not impede India's economic, political and historical integration. Religious tolerance was a rule rather than exception, in the feudal empires of the Muslim rulers and in the states of Hindu *rajas*. This is not to state that feudal India had no outbreaks of reaction or religious persecution (certainly not the case with the regime of Aurangzeb). However, religious intolerance, usually, was a concomitant of the decay of the feudal order and not at all typical of the pre-colonial period as a whole.[67]

Differences of religion also coincided with class and caste differences. It is notable that assimilation of the Muslim conquerors with the indigenous Hindu population resulted in a remarkable reciprocity between Hinduism and Islam. The bulk of Muslims were evidently converts form Hinduism, especially from the lower strata. The socio-economic disparity inherent in this socio-historic mobilization was later exploited skillfully in communal terms by the British colonialists. That religious differences did not matter when resistance to colonial enslavement was called for, was amply demonstrated by the united Hindu-Muslim rebellion of 1857. The colonial masters were shrewd enough to sense this. The result was a carefully designed policy of *divide et impera*, meticulously implemented in the subsequent century. As mentioned earlier, the colonialists also succeeded in giving a religious complexion to the social contradictions in the country.

It is important to recall that following the rebellion of 1857 the Muslims were initially targeted as the deadly enemy, but a few years later, to counter the growing popularity of the Indian National Congress, the same colonialists blessed the formation of the Muslim League, hailing "the Nobles, Jagirdars, Taluqdars, Zamindars, Lawyers and Merchants, subjects of His Majesty, the King-Emperor in different parts of India", as possessing a "representative character". For the imperial state the achievement was "nothing less than the pulling back of sixty-two millions of people from joining the ranks of the seditious opposition."[68] The design was clear. The Muslim League was rewarded with separate electorates and positive discrimination in state employment for its unflinching loyalty to the empire. The Muslim elite embraced with open arms the coveted privileges offered by the colonial state and opposed, in the beginning, the principle of competitive entry into the civil services, and later all proposals of equality on almost any level. Since the property rights and socio-political privileges of this class depended on the state, it was to foster concrete theo-political moves through increasing alliance with the British civil servants.

The colonial state's carefully designed venture to institutionalize a communal demand in the infancy of the Indian national liberation movement exposed its intriguing predilections and paved the way for a communal-separatist movement in the subsequent decades. It has been aptly commented: "... since without separate electorates there surely would have been no Pakistan, it might well have been, who knows, the case of losing a war for want of a horse-shoe."[69] In that case, there was a possibility that if "the British had not colonized and ruled India for nearly fifteen decades, the confessional state of Pakistan would not have come into existence on 14 August, 1947."[70]

The calculated divisive designs of the imperialists to counter the nationalists are well documented in Indian historiography dealing with the freedom struggle. It also needs to be borne in mind that the strategy of divisive politics of the imperialists was skillfully coupled with their social conservatism, that contributed towards political dormance of the large mass of the convention-ridden, status quoist, unaware social universe. It is true that the Congress also fell short of effectively containing both Muslim communalism and Hindu extremism, despite Gandhi's intensive and extensive project of constructive programme. It was not fully grasped that communal politics was also, in significant ways, a distorted reflection of social, economic and regional disparities. Socio-economic development could not attain top priority on the agenda of either the Congress or the League, and least of all, of the colonial state, which was expectedly preoccupied with its own survival at all costs. Moreover, politics in a colonial situation, more specifically in the first quarter of the twentieth century India, was dominated by the upper and upper middle classes in urban centres, providing possible leverage to the theo-political manoeuvres of the vested propertied interests.

Islam was used as a mobilizing strategy by the League, transcending all socio-economic disparities. The strategy proved efficacious in presenting the interests of the leaders as the interests of the Muslim masses, which was certainly not the case. The Muslim intelligentsia was also confronted with dilemmas of theo-political initiatives, supremely evidenced by the poet-philosopher, Iqbal. The poet who was, and is still, venerated for the secular nationalist *Tarana-i-Hind and Naya Shivala* began to talk of the desirability of a separate homeland for Muslims, forcefully presented in his 1930 presidential address to the Muslim League at Allahabad.

In the meantime, attempts by the Congress and the Muslim League to reach consensus on a Constitution for India foundered due to political mistrust, as illustrated by the confrontationist stances adopted by both on Nehru Report and Jinnah's 'Fourteen Point Proposal'. To worsen matters, 'politics from the above' in the form of Round Table Conferences and proposals for constitutional reforms continued to widen the hiatus between the two organizations and the communities. The non-communal social reality of India, below the surface of artificial political cleavages, was obscured and callously neglected.

The League persisted with its claims of exclusively representing the Muslims and branded the Congress as a 'Hindu body'. In March 1940, Jinnah openly asked Gandhi to "come as a Hindu leader proudly representing your people and let me meet you proudly representing the Musalmans?"[71] Jinnah knew very well that he was expecting the impossible. And, without using the word 'Pakistan', he played his final trump card through the Lahore Resolution, declaring that the "problem in India is not of an inter-communal but manifestly of an international character, and it must be treated as such... the only course open to us all is to allow the major nations separate homelands by dividing India into autonomous national states." All through the subsequent years, Jinnah remained adamant on two points, viz., complete parity with the Congress, and recognition of the right of the Muslims to Pakistan in any future constitutional settlement. With the launching of the Quit India Movement in 1942, as the Congress grew increasingly hostile to the British empire, the League gained in proximity to the latter. The embittered Gandhi strongly demanded on June 11, 1942, "the final departure of the colonialists and said... "the third power, even without deliberately wishing it, will not allow real unity to take place."[72]

Jinnah and the League, however, condemned Gandhi and the Quit India Movement as an attempt "to force the Musalmans to submit and surrender to Congress terms and dictation." And ultimately Jinnah succeeded in "swaying opinion" in his favour. Consequently, the Gandhi-Jinnah talks, the last straw in the strong sea, proved a futile exercise. Gandhi felt the whole idea of two-nation theory was "absurd" and "wholly unreal". He categorically asserted: "I find no parallel in history for a body of converts and their descendants, claiming to be a nation apart from the parent stock. If India was one nation before the advent of Islam, it must remain one in spite of the change of faith of a very large body of her children."[73]

Gandhi could not accept this "new test of nationhood", lest it should lead to "an insoluble problem". The prophetic words of Gandhi were not heeded to at that time, though truly vindicated when Islam could not prevent 'Bengalis' to secede from Pakistan, in less than two and a half decades of the creation of the sacred homeland for believers in Islam. The movements for 'four nationalities' and now for the 'fifth nationality' in contemporary Pakistan further vindicated Gandhi's argument. Gandhi's indictment of the imperial power was equally final: "... the presence of a third power hinders the solution. *A mind enslaved cannot act as if it was free*"[74] (emphasis added).

Gandhi was referring to the irreparable harm the imperial state had done to the psyche and the consciousness of the 'colonized'. The malaise was deeper than visible on the surface. However ironical as it may sound, Jinnah did not completely rule out a federal solution till 1946, although 1937 onwards he had been persistently harping on the separatist ideology. This should explain his ambivalent response to Gandhi when the latter conceded in 1944 in a pensive mood: "Let it be a partition as between two brothers, if a division there must be." Wolpert has rightly commented that Jinnah's angry rejection when Gandhi seemed ready to endorse Pakistan, appears to indicate that Jinnah really wanted no part in negotiating a formal settlement with the Congress and was caught off guard by Gandhi's swift last moment reversal of position.[75] It is notable that more than anything else, Gandhi's 'reversal of position' was motivated by his life-time ideal of communal amity between Hindus and Muslims. An incorrigible optimist, as he was, Gandhi still hoped for a 'change of heart' of 'brother Jinnah', though it did not take him long to be disillusioned with his own optimism.

Ultimately, the creation of Pakistan was a story of the success of the theo-political manoeuvres of communalist forces, with blessings of the pragmatic colonial state.[76] As for the Indian masses—Hindus and Muslims—the creation of Pakistan was, indeed, the end of an illusion and also the beginning of another.[77] Preceding and following the partition, Gandhi's 'pilgrimage' to the riot-ridden areas of human jungle in Calcutta, Noakhali and Bihar, reinforced the fact that brute force and its transient success was but an impoverished substitute for the unflinching human spirit, even when there was ruinous devastation all around. In the frenzy of indiscriminate violence, Gandhi's ideals were shattered for a while, yet it was Gandhi alone, who could be described as "one man boundary force." Appropriately, Mountbatten acknowledged gratefully "what fifty thousand well-equipped soldiers could not do, the Mahatma had done."[78]

It is a historical irony that M.A. Jinnah, the fiery crusader for theo-national separatism in pre-partitioned India, advocated a secular state for Pakistan in his very first speech to the Constituent Assembly of Pakistan on August 11, 1947.[79] He persisted with his advocacy till death, but with no political impact in the new state.

As for Gandhi, he had certainly, not failed with the masses. His symbols were not betrayed by the public consciousness. His trust was betrayed by the politicians. Also, his failure on the communal front was probably an ill-conceived and mismanaged political fall-out of the colonial situation. His notion of 'principled praxis' was betrayed, yet paradoxically it was precisely the desertion of the 'rules of the game' that was later lamented. True, Gandhi's symbols were partly misrepresented and partly rejected, yet Gandhi himself became the most resonant symbol of the suffering masses of colonial India and their anti-imperialist struggle.

Another grave social problem that needed to be grappled with, for substantial *swaraj*, was gender inequality in Indian society. Women were oppressed in innumerable ways in India. They were voiceless, disempowered and absolutely marginalized. They had no autonomy in their personal lives and no role in the public life of the nation. Gandhi had the remarkable insight to interrelate the two and reconstruct an alternative image of Indian women, at once 'emancipated' in their personal and social lives and 'committed' to the nationalist cause of political liberation. And, he succeeded not wholly, but to a large extent.

As discussed earlier, philosophically speaking, Gandhi's theory of social transformation is largely premised on the cardinal assumptions of *advaita*, precluding all forms of discriminatory practices and values between man and man, and man and woman. Gender equality is, thus, inherently implicit in his fundamental premises of social transformation. Admittedly, the philosophy of *advaita* has been reconciled in practice with a highly discriminatory social system in India for approximately one thousand years. Gandhi was not unaware of the advertent/inadvertent misinterpretations and misappropriations of the basic postulates of Vedic and Vedantic philosophy by vested interests. He castigated such attempts in strongest terms, time and again. But, at the same time, he remained assured of the perennial principles and, persistently reinterpreted and improvised the same in terms of practical relevance, invariably employing them as a philosophico-normative reference point and a justificatory theory for the social transformation of his vision. Viewed thus, the question of gender equality in the Gandhian framework is that of qualitative and meaningful change in the direction of genuine freedom, equality and dignity for women.

Gandhi visualized a radically transformed egalitarian society in which the natural differences between man and woman are not transformed into hierarchical opposition but rather co-exist fruitfully with their common concerns and sensibilities. It is pertinent to recall that Gandhi, preceded by Gokhale and Ram Mohan Roy, long before the feminist movement gained ground in India, launched a powerful and a radical assault on the central institutions and values of patriarchy, the social mindset of men and women and the oppressive structures in India society. He persuasively argued that the roots of gender discrimination lay much deeper than generally realized, "in man's greed of power and fame and deeper still in mutual lust."[80] He, therefore, exhorted young women to confront and defy the patriarchal norms in deciding important matters concerning themselves, such as the matters of marriage, of children, of equal rights. In his view, "if the husband is a god the wife is also a goddess. She is not a slave, but a friend and companion with equal rights."[81] He also advocated women's rights of separation and remarriage in case of discord and injustice. Gandhi not only questioned but also rejected the contemporary throttling customs and religious taboos and notions of false morality. This was an act of empowering woman in the domestic space. Being an adherent of *Brahmacharya*, Gandhi urged for sexual self-restraint for both men and women.[82] Accordingly, he did not favour remarriage of widows and widowers. However, when he saw persistence of widower remarriage, justified for a number of reasons, he started advocating widow remarriage as well, on principles of equality and justice.[83]

True at times, Gandhi appeared to be strongly conservative in his glorification of certain 'feminine' qualities of women, as 'naturally' different from men.[84] Yet, it is obvious that he did not believe in the traditional stereotypes of the nature and roles of men and women, when we look at what he expected them to do and helped them in doing so. In fact, he worked hard to breakdown stereotypes about the nature and the consequent roles of men and women in society. In his efforts to demolish the stereotypes in India, Gandhi urged women to cultivate the qualities of courage, self-assertion and self-determination through participation in the national liberation movement. The creed of non-violence, the foundation of the *satyagraha* struggle, as Gandhi interpreted it, demanded that men cultivate qualities hitherto considered as feminine. He also sought to invert the traditional division of roles between men and women by requiring menfolk in his *ashrams* to take part in cooking, serving food, cleaning, etc., so long considered to be the duties of women and below male dignity.

It is little acknowledged that in his radical critique of Hindu scriptures and social customs, Gandhi was much ahead of his times in attacking patriarchy in both institutional and normative terms. He castigated parents forcing "marriage on their daughters"[85] and keeping the latter "unfit for earning their living". Gandhi also questioned the age-old practices, such as the practice of *kanyadan* (giving away the daughter in marriage): "Has a father any rights of property over his children ? He is their protector not owner. And he forfeits the privilege of protection when he abuses it by seeking to barter away the liberty of his ward."[86] He was equally categorical in his condemnation of marriages arranged for money and rightly diagnosed that the system was "intimately connected with caste."[87] So long as the choice was restricted to a few hundred young men and young women of a particular caste, he argued, the system would persist. "The girls or boys or their parents will have to break the bonds of caste if the evil is to be eradicated... All this means education of a character that will revolutionize the mentality of the youth of the nation."[88]

Gandhi vociferously argued that a "strong public opinion should be created in condemnation of the degrading practice of dowry and young men who soil their fingers with such ill-gotten gold should be excommunicated from society."[89] "A real property," he insisted, "that a parent can transmit to all equally is his or her character and educational facilities. Parents should seek to make their sons and daughters self-reliant, well able to earn an honest livelihood by the sweat of the brow."[90]

Surprisingly, Gandhi outpaced many reformers and feminists, when he argued that what was uppermost in the crusade for gender-equality was "to free woman from mental slavery, to teach her the sacredness of her body and to teach her the dignity of national service and the service of humanity."[91] He exhorted women "to learn the primary right of resistance."[92] Almost half a century later, the feminists, questioning the prevailing model of medical technology, are arguing likewise, although they do not share the Gandhian argument of unqualified primacy of nationalism and humanism.

It is pertinent to bear in mind that Gandhi was not wedded to mere intellectual diagnoses and theoretical analyses of problems. He was primarily an activist, who practised what he preached, and a crusader, who fought for what he believed to be the just cause. Above all, he was a radical reformer who believed in the necessity as well as the possibility of self-generated social transformation. Accordingly, he visualized women as active subjects and not the objects in social and national revolution.

Significantly, anticipating radical feminists, Gandhi elucidated that women "are labouring under the hypnotic influence of man..." However, he emphasized, that "if they would realize the strength of non-violence, they would not consent to be called the weaker sex.[93] For meaningful social transformation, women also need "to refuse to be the slaves of their own whims and fancies and the slaves of men."[94] He was again radically ahead of his times, in his curt warning: "Man, the law giver, will have to pay a dreadful penalty for the degradation he has imposed upon the so-called weaker sex. When woman, freed from man's snares, rises to the full height and rebels against man's legislation and institutions designed by him, her rebellion, no doubt non-violent, will be nonetheless effective."[95] "As women begin to realize their strength," he reiterated, "as they must in proportion to the education they receive, they will naturally resent the glaring inequalities to which they are subjected."[96] Gandhi, therefore, strongly urged women "to resort to civil rebellion against all undesirable and unworthy restraints."[97] This was to be the real foundation of self-transformation and emancipation for them. Gandhi also disapproved of patronage. He clearly stated, "women, and for that matter any group should disdain patronage. They should seek justice, never favours".[98] However, he added: "seeing... that it has been the custom to decry women, the contrary custom should be to prefer women, merit being equal, to men even if the preference should result in men being entirely displaced by women."[99]

Gandhi was sceptical about the strategy of the feminists,

"crying out for women's rights" as he described the phenomenon. Instead, he urged "the enlightened women of India to deal with the root cause of gender injustice "to spot and eradicate age-old evils."[100] He also exhorted women activists to "enrol women as voters, impart or have imparted to them practical education, teach them to think independently, release them from the chains of caste that bind them, so as to bring about a change in them which will compel men to realize woman's strength and capacity for sacrifice and give her place of honour.[101] These strategies, rather than sloganeering, would go a long way in both emancipating and empowering women, in his view.

Gandhi repeatedly enjoined that "woman should feel as independent as man. Bravery is not man's monopoly". Women in Gandhi's view, may not look for protection to men. They must rely on their own strength and purity of character and on God.[102] In Gandhi's view, strength is not physical but moral power, and in that, he insisted, "woman is immeasurably man's superior," and therefore "more fitted than man to make explorations and take bolder action in *ahimsa*."[103] Gandhi visualized woman to be the unquestioned leader in a non-violent revolution. He exalted woman as an incarnation of *ahimsa*, that also implied infinite love and went as far as saying: "Let her transfer that love to the whole of humanity.... It is given to her to teach the art of peace to the warring world thirsting for that nectar."[104] Thus, in Gandhi's conception, woman had a role to play not merely in the domestic and social spheres but also at national and the global levels.

Gender revolution has to be a multifaceted struggle, involving a number of strategies. Gandhi underscored education as the key to gender revolution. No qualitative, meaningful social change was conceivable without education among women. Notably, Gandhi advocated co-education right from his South African days. He also advocated sex-education for children at an appropriate age. The real objective of education, in his view, ought to be to enable women to be fearless, self-confident and self-dependent. Accordingly, he urged for displacing and dispensing with the stereotype of woman as delicate, weak and timid. There is no substitute for courage, fearlessness and self-determination in the Gandhian scheme of social revolution.

Gandhi sought to go beyond the traditional images of women as *devi* (goddess) *mangla* (auspicious) *samrajni* (empress), and rejected the degenerated *bhogya* (sex object) image. He incited women to emerge as a self-confident, self-reliant and self-disciplined identity. His own improvised image of woman was that of a *sakhi* (friend), with unlimited reservoir of moral power (*shakti*), *ahimsa*, self-sacrifice and perseverance. Gandhi's alternative feminine image drew upon the rich symbolism sustained in Indian cultural tradition in the role images of Sita, Draupadi, and Damyanti invoked for courage and righteousness, simplicity, and indomitable will.

Invoking the imperatives of *swadharma* and *nishkam karma* (dispassionate action) of the *Gita*, Gandhi ruminated: "whoever works according to her capacity has fulfilled her mission. But why should they [women] not extend the field of their ministry so as to embrace the whole of India...? Where service is rendered to the country consistently with the welfare of the world it finally leads to self-realization."[105]

As discussed earlier, it is pertinent to bear in mind that as Gandhi was historically situated in the colonial context, his crusade for social transformation was an integral part of the struggle for political independence. Social regeneration in the Gandhian agenda was coextensive with moral and political regeneration. In fact, grass-root movement was to be the *terra firma* on which the edifice of swaraj of his vision could be built.

There was no other way of raising mass consciousness in the given historical context. And, it was to Gandhi's credit, that his call brought forth massive support and participation not only of common men but also of common women. Indian women, for the first time in national history, volunteered to enter the mainstream of national struggle, pledged to fulfil the honourable obligation. Agreeably, the focus in the given situation was on nationalism and social regeneration, not on feminism. This was in keeping with the spirit of the times. Yet, it was to be the beginning of a social revolution. Though Gandhi's innovative experiment of social emancipation through political mobilization could not ensure gender equality in the social arena as he had visualized, it did nevertheless prove to be a milestone in kindling a new spirit and a radical resolve to challenge entrenched inhibitions and constricted perspectives.

Gandhi specifically drew upon the symbolism of *charkha* and *khadi* to involve women in the national mainstream. Historically recalling that two hundred years ago, the women of India spun not only for home demand but also for foreign lands, Gandhi argued that in order to solve the problem of mass poverty in India, reintroduction of the spinning wheel was essential. Boycott of foreign clothes/articles was another strategy, as much political as psychological. Women had a key role to play in the above strategy by both abdicating their own love for foreign finery and socializing their families to do likewise. Apart from enlivening the *swadeshi* spirit, women also performed onerous service to the cause of the removal of untouchability and of forging communal amity. In the political struggle, women played a notable role, specifically in the Civil Disobedience Movement and later Quit India Movement. Dharsana *satyagraha* became the high watermark not only of large scale participation, courage and sacrifice of women, but also their effective leadership. Campaigns for prohibition and picketing of liquor and foreign cloth shops were efficaciously carried out by women in large numbers. This was an entirely new agenda for women, uncharted and unprecedented, to act not only as equal partners, but also as initiators of leading roles. And Indian women emerged with flying colours in trying times of travails and tribulations. Gandhi's leadership notably enthused confidence, trust and determination among the people of India—men and women alike. This was the kind of ardour that was essential for social regeneration in an inverse political milieu.

Gandhi realized that the issue of gender equality was a very sensitive issue, in the given Indian ethos. The objective presupposed as much an external mode of struggle as "reform from within", that is, change in the mindset of both men and women. Parity of sexes needed to be accepted without ignoring their natural differences. However, Gandhi cautioned against misinterpreting parity as 'mimicking' of man by woman. "She can run the race," he said, "but she will not rise to the great heights she is capable of by mimicking man."[106]

Correspondingly, far from supporting the superiority of male-centred civilization, Gandhi exalted the superiority of the feminine. Notably, the exaltation was neither a political stance nor a populist stratagem but absolutely in keeping with his vision of a non-violent and just socio-political order. Time and again, he reiterated "...If non-violence is the law of our being the future is with woman..."[107]

Madhu Kishwar rightly points out that "Gandhi repeatedly dismissed the more situationally relevant Rani of Jhansi symbol in favour of a combination Sita-Draupadi symbol whereby answers were sought not primarily in a woman's individual strength and the way to cultivate it but in the realm of women's spiritual and moral courage. His choice of a certain kind of feminine courage in preference to other kinds of strength and heroism reflects his vision which was one of women acting primarily as the best exemplars of a certain moral force in society."[108] As mentioned earlier, this vision was a logical corollary of his ideal of a non-violent egalitarian social order.

Gandhi's vision of social reconstruction, thus, envisages a simultaneous emancipation of the individual (man and woman) and the society. It is an advocacy for ensuring autonomy of the individual within the reciprocity of the community. As the interrelationship between the two has been decisively determined by cultural/traditional codes, norms, structures, Gandhi is in favour of addressing culture and tradition, squarely. A wholesale rejection of culture and tradition in neither feasible nor desirable. Therefore, in Gandhi's view, the cultural heritage and tradition need to be reclaimed through reinterpretation, renovation and adaptation to the needs of the times. Innovative experiments are also not precluded. At the same time, Gandhi is not hesitant in challenging, even inverting the hegemonic, oppressive socio-cultural structures/norms, that have been instrumental in creating and sustaining an inegalitarian and unjust social order. In this regard, Gandhi's constructive programme, as an alternative strategy is specifically notable for generating enormous social energy needed for a radical restructuring of social relations. And, although Gandhi's achievement might not have been a resounding success but he did succeed in bringing the deep-seated schisms of Indian society on the national agenda, to be seriously addressed and confronted.

Notes

1. *Young India*, June 12, 1924, p.195.

2. M.K. Gandhi, *Constructive Programme: Its Meaning and Place*, Ahmedabad, Navajivan, 1945, p.7.
3. *CWMG*, Vol. XXIV, p.33.
4. Ashis Nandy, *At The Edge of Psychology: Essays in Politics and Culture*, Delhi, Oxford University, Press, 1980, p.71.
5. Irfan Habib, "Gandhi and the National Movement," *Social Scientist*, 23, 4-6, April-June 1995, p.8.
6. *CWMG*, vol. XXVII, p.308.
7. *CWMG*, vol. XXV, p.536.
8. Irfan Habib, *Note 5*, p.9.
9. S. Radhakrishnan, *The Bhagwad Gita*, London, George Allen & Unwin, 1970, p.66 and 137.
10. Mahadev Desai, *The Gospel of Selfless Action or the Gita According to Gandhi*, Ahmedabad, Navajivan, 1956, pp.131 & 133.
11. *Harijan*, March 25, 1939, p.64.
12. *Note 11.*
13. *Note 2.*
14. See, M.K. Gandhi, *Satyagraha in South Africa* (Trans. V.G. Desai) Ahmedabad, Navajivan (1928), 1993.
15. G.N. Dhawan, *The Political Philosophy of Mahatma Gandhi*, New Delhi, Gandhi Peace Foundation, 1990, p.192.
16. Richard B. Gregg, *The Power of Non-Violence*, Ahmedabad, Navajivan, 1960, p.306.
17. *Harijan*, September 9, 1937, p.292.
18. *Harijan*, September 19, 1947, p.379.
19. *Harijan*, December 21, 1947, p.476.
20. *Harijan*, September 21, 1934, p.253.
21. *Young India*, September 13, 1921, p.325.
22. *Note* 2, p.11.
23. *Young India*, July 21, 1920, p.4.
24. *Young India*, September 20, 1921, p.329.
25. *Young India*, September 17, 1925, p.321.
26. *Young India*, June 18, 1925, p.211.
27. *Young India*, August 27, 1925, p.299.

28. *Harijan*, April 27, 1934, p.85.
29. *Young India*, February 8, 1921, p.406.
30. *Harijan*, April 13, 1940, p.85.
31. M.K. Gandhi, *Khadi: Why and How*, Ahmedabad, Navajivan, (1955) 1959, pp. 181 & 185.
32. *Note* 2, pp.12-13.
33. *CWMG*, Vol. XXV, p.356.
34. *CWMG*, Vol. XXVII, p.32.
35. M.K. Gandhi, *From Yervada Mandir*, Ahmedabad, Navajivan, 1957, p.44.
36. *SW*, Vol. V, p. 444.
37. *CWMG*, Vol. XIX, p. 289.
38. *Note* 35, p.31.
39. *Note* 36, p.341.
40. *Harijan*, September 28, 1934, p.261.
41. *CWMG*, Vol. LVI, p.246, and Vol. XXXV, pp. 1-3, 105-7, 259-63.
42. Ramashray Roy, *Self and Society: A Study in Gandhian Thought*, New Delhi, Sage, 1984, p.70.
43. *Note* 35, p.32.
44. *Note* 35, p.33.
45. *CWMG*, Vol. LXVI, pp. 35-36.
46. *Note* 45, p.42.
47. *CWMG*, LXIV, p.243.
48. D.G. Tendulkar, *Mahatma* Vol. III, p.128.
49. *Note* 48, p.163.
50. Denis Dalton, "The Gandhian View of Caste and Caste After Gandhi" in P. Mason (ed.), *India and Ceylon: Unity and Diversity*, London, Oxford University Press, 1960, p. 175
51. H.S. Polak, H.N. Brailsford and Lord Pethick Lawrence, *Mahatma Gandhi*, London, Odhams Press, 1949, p.208.
52. *Note* 35, p.38.

    Also See, *Young India*, May 29, 1924, p.180.
53. *Note* 35, pp.39-40.

54. M.K. Gandhi, *My Religion* (ed. Bharatan Kumarappa), Ahmedabad, Navajivan, (1955) 1985, p.30.
55. *Note* 54, p.29.
56. *Harijan*, November 28, 1936, p.330.
57. *Young India*, August 11, 1920, p.3.
58. *Young India*, December 20, 1928, p.420.
59. *Young India*, December 20, 1928, p.420.
60. See *Harijan*, June 8, 1935, p.132.
61. *Harijan*, October 13, 1946, p.357.
62. *Young India*, September 24, 1925, pp.331-32.
63. *Young India*, June 10, 1926, p.211.
64. *Harijan*, April 28, 1946, p.111.
65. *Young India*, October 6, 1921, p.318.
66. Chaudhari Muhammad Ali, *The Emergence of Pakistan*, New York, Columbia University Press, 1967, pp.29-30.
67. *Hind Swaraj* (1909), Ahmedabad, Navajivan, 1938, pp. 44-49.
68. See, Mary, Countess of Minto, *India, Minto and Morley, 1905-10*, Macmillan, 1934, pp.47-48, quoted in S. Wolpert, *Jinnah of Pakistan*, Delhi, Oxford, 1985, p.24.
69. Sharif-al-Mujahid, *Quaid-i-Azam Jinnah: Studies in Interpretation*, Karachi, Quaid-i-Azam Academy, 1981, p.13.
70. Tariq Ali, *Can Pakistan Survive? The Death of a State*, Harmondsworth, Penguin Books, 1983, p.15.
71. S.S. Pirzada (ed.) *Foundations of Pakistan: All India Muslim League Documents*, Vol. II, Karachi, National Publishing House, 1969, pp.332-33.
72. *CWMG*, Vol. LXXVI, p.213.
73. *CWMG*, Vol. LXXVIII, p.101.
74. *Note* 73, pp.136-37.
75. Stanley Wolpert, *Jinnah of Pakistan*, Delhi, Oxford University Press, 1985, p.70.
76. See for details, Asha Kaushik and S.N. Kaushik, "Religion as Political Ideology: The Separatist Crusade of Jinnah," *South Asian Studies*, 29, 2, July-December, 1994, pp.1-10.

77. See A. Kaushik, "Creation of Pakistan: Ideological Ambivalence of Theo-Politics," *South Asian Studies*, 31, 1 & 2, January-December 1996, pp. 100-112.
78. M.K. Gandhi, *Correspondence with the Government: 1944-47*, Ahmedabad, Navajivan, 1959, p.277.
79. *Jinnah: Speeches as Governor General of Pakistan: 1947-48*, Karachi, Government of Pakistan Publication, n.d., pp.8-9.
80. *Young India*, October 17, 1929, p.340.
81. *The Diary of Mahadev Desai*, I (Trans. & ed. V.G. Desai), Ahmedabad, Navajivan, 1953, p.189.
82. 'Sexlessness' in terms of absolute sexual restraint, was Gandhi's ideal for both the sexes. It was not a prejudiced patriarchal advocacy in disfavour of women as Madhu Kishwar and Sujata Patel argue. See for details, Madhu Kishwar 'Gandhi on Women' *Economic and Political Weekly*, October 5, 1985, pp. 1691-1702, and S. Patel, 'Construction and Reconstruction of Woman in Gandhi', *EPW*, February 20, 1988, pp. 377-387.
83. *Note 82*, p.107.
84. See, for criticism of Gandhi on this point, M. Kishwar and S. Patel *Note 82*.
85. *Harijan*, September 15, 1946, pp. 311-12.
86. *Young India*, November 11, 1926, p.388.
87. *Harijan*, May 23, 1936, p.117.
88. *Note 87*.
89. *Young India*, June 21, 1928, p.207.
90. *Note 80*.
91. *Harijan*, May 2, 1936, p.396.
92. *Harijan*, Jan 25, 1936, p.396.
93. *Young India*, January 14, 1932, p.19.
94. *Young India*, December 8, 1927, p.406.
95. *Young India*, April 16, 1925, p.133.
96. *Note 80*.
97. *Harijan*, March 23, 1947, p.80.
98. *Harijan*, April 7, 1946, p.67.
99. *Note 98*.

100. *Note 80.*
101. *Harijan*, April 21, 1946, p.96.
102. *Harijan*, September 15, 1947, p.80.
103. *Young India*, April 10, 1930, p.121.
104. *Harijan*, February 24, 1940, pp. 13-14.
105. *Note 36*, p.430.
106. *Harijan*, February 27, 1937, p.19.
107. *Young India*, April 10, 1930, p.121.
108. *Note 82*, p.1692.

6

Summation

> "I want the cultures of all lands to be blown about my house as freely as possible. But I refuse to be blown off my feet by any."[1]

If the objective of "true philosophy is to learn again to see the world" as Merleau-Ponty states, the salience of Gandhian philosophy is ascertainable precisely in these terms. The formidable objective of 'learning again' involves as much 'unlearning' as 'learning anew'. Gandhian thought, therefore, is comprehensible as a simultaneous endeavour at 'deconstructing' the prevalent modes of theorizing and praxis and 'reconstructing' an alternative mode. Primarily concerned with rendering socio-political life intelligible, Gandhian political thought is not insulated in any metaphysical sense, but profoundly engaged with concrete sufferings and predicaments of people.

Focussing on colonial India's concrete politico-economic exploitation and psycho-social oppression, Gandhi ventures to ask how the shift in perspective—from the received western worldview to a 'rooted' point of view—might alter the fundamental categories, methodology and self-understanding of a society, in its own setting and relatedness to the outer world. Gandhian worldview is a 'displacement' of the logic of the modern western paradigm of 'growth-progress-modernization' and 'replacement' of the same by an Indian civilizational argument for an egalitarian-communitarian order. The significance of Gandhian framework lies in this paradigm shift.

It is not to argue here that Gandhi's Indian civilizational 'project' is an axiomatic harbinger of universal freedom, happiness or peace. Gandhi is realist enough not to be satisfied with rigid categories of antitheses, in either political or cultural terms. At the same time, he is aware of the perils of moving briskly beyond them. What Gandhi attempts, therefore, is a serious interrogation of prevailing structures of domination/exploitation and their justicafory theories, whether western or eastern. It is, in no way, an argument favouring 'clashes of civilizations'.[2] But certainly, it is an argument necessitating a reconsideration of a human being's relationships with other human beings, with the world and with nature—a reconsideration that conjures up the dangers of objectivism and naturalism. Although seemingly esoteric at times, Gandhi's sketched assessment of our age is, therefore, significantly pertinent to contemporary intellectual and political controversies and pinpoints alternative directions of politico-economic order.

In his attempt at radical questioning and renewal, Gandhi, through his devised symbolism, captures the innermost thrust of Indian civilization, relying on the active moral/social character of subjectivity and the constitutive role of consciousness along with a faith in communitarian reciprocity. As if sharing the afflictions of philosophy, Gandhi shuns all premature pretensions to knowledge/understanding and insists on constant experimentation to get nearer an understanding of truth, as a scientist would. Gandhi is remarkably optimistic about the power of the human spirit and its potential to think and move boldly on uncharted paths. Accordingly, he sets out daringly in some new directions sometimes, though at others he prefers to stay more losely near the border of the time-honoured politico-cultural experience. The latter position probably vindicates his moorings, rather than a fear of the unknown or distrust in human capabilities. In fact, Gandhi, like Plato, enquires about the basic purpose of life and comes up with an answer in terms of human-perfectibility. And, in consonance with Kant, he upholds the dignity of each human-being as an end in itself.

Gandhi rejects the utilitarian calculus of liberal political theory and its glorification of atomistic individualism, "not founded upon the relations between man and man but rather upon the separation of man from man" as Marx argues. Gandhi's alternative theory of political obligation regards liberty as much a *duty* as a right. It is premised on rational-moral action. Rational-moral action, in Gandhian paradigm is God (truth/humanity)-dedicated activity (*karmyoga*), which is selfless in essence. The discontinuities and the asymmetry between political morality and personal morality, so assiduously ingrained in modern consciousness, is overcome in Gandhi's radical ethic. On this score, as on many others, Gandhian thought provides us an image for the oddity of our situation and an alternative perception.

Gandhi's is a normative conception of humanity derived from *advaita*. In the west, Plato, Rousseau, Kant, even Marx have talked likewise. According to this view, the uniqueness of the individual coexists with his place in humankind, which inheres in him in his individuality, however large the totality of humankind may be. It is in him that the humanity has its immediate language and existence. It is a unitive vision, born of spiritual communion and identification with all human beings, in fact, all living beings. This reality lends humanity the whole boundless breadth of its phenomena, the particular within the general as its existential character and vice versa. This also applies to the identity of cultures, in whose constancy, not in their levelling out, lies the 'value content' of the whole. The tensions arising between various forms of identities are resolved in Gandhian thought in the conceptualization of Oceanic Circles. The normative conception is remarkably translated into an ideology of emancipation of the individual, the nation, as well as the global community.

A liberated individual, society or humanity, will be intrinsically moral for Gandhi. No action can be moral which is not voluntary. Any action dictated by fear or coercion would be violent and cease to be moral. Non-violence, that is, freedom from fear and coercion, is the essence of Gandhi's alternative paradigm of emancipation, and indeed, of true *swaraj*. Given the logic of the convertibility of means and ends, violent means must result in a vicious circle of violence, which can be counteracted only through non-violence. Convictions of morality and non-violence become practiceable only through an identification with the whole of mankind. In Gandhi's view, political activity provides a forum for such identification. Needless to repeat, such conviction is premised on Gandhi's alternative conceptualization of the nature of politics itself.

Gandhi had immense faith in the human potential for goodness and morality. He believed that men were not merely material creatures but were capable of higher ends and modes of thinking, feeling and acting. They were capable of even dying for causes opposed to their material interests. It is on the basis of this belief that Gandhi succeeded in imparting the message of 'protest as *swadharma*' (duty) to people from every nook and corner of India. Consequently, much more than a political act, protest became a matter of deep conviction.

Gandhi could not accept the argument of the invincibility of the imperial regime or inevitability of the industrial model or superiority of the western civilization. Gandhi questioned not merely the 'how' of the liberal-industrial combine but also the 'why' of their superimpositions on the non-west. Gandhi's critique of the western paradigm is both theoretical and practical. He questions the glorification of reason and of hedonism as the hall-mark of material betterment, as both serve as the bed-rock of western industrial-capitalist urban civilization.[3]

The objective for Gandhi is good life. True, the growth-modernization model has to its credit, enormous acquisitive attainments, but also a constantly shrinking space of human and normative concerns. Ironically, the betterment of life, in terms of rising material standards of living, has often resulted in eroding the foundations of good life, through a lopsided emphasis on material accomplishments and hedonism. Extending to the politico-economic and cultural spheres, the phenomenon has been instrumental in creating structures of domination, with both hegemonizing and homogenizing traits. Increasing rationality, as Habermas notes, has not enhanced understanding of the self and others.[4] Likewise, increasing materialism in Gandhi's view, is no indication of human well-being. Gandhi's strong recommendation of moral reasoning should be taken as a necessary corrective to obsession with economism and what Marcuse describes as 'instrumental reason'/rationality.

However, Gandhi's 'civilizational critique' of the west is not a romantic declaration of war on the consequences of progress. Gandhi's revolt is against its political essence and the spiralling politico-economic ambitions.[5] Gandhi's struggle for moral and politico-economic regeneration, therefore, remains a simultaneous endeavour. The argument of the inexorable process of economic growth and progress, has been distinctively built on faith in the emancipatory potential of science and technology. On this point, there is a remarkable consensus between the liberals and the Marxists. True, as Noble has rightly commented, whereas the capitalists apologized for and rallied behind technological progress, the socialists revered it.[6] Gandhi, on the other hand, remained most skeptical about the emancipatory role of technology, in the given politico-economic set up. As if pre-empting Adorno and Marcuse, he castigated the employment of technology for objectives of domination and exploitation. His moral critique was also always there. Gandhi's critique of technology, however, was not absolute. As an alternative to the gigantic, awe-inspiring presence of technology, Gandhi visualized a decentralized form of technology, suitable for the local needs of the people. The small in this sense was not only beautiful for him but also humane. Gandhi, therefore, is not anti-technological, *per se*, but a votary of need-oriented, appropriate technology, subordinate to human ends rather than 'technicist' developmentalism.

If it is not untrue that humane standards of behaviour evolve paradoxically at times when relations among races and people become particularly inhuman, Gandhi's optimism and crusade for a more humane world would not seem to be unfounded or untenable. At one level, Gandhi sought to radicalize the prevailing patterns of morality by bringing in its purview the social factors that decisively mediate its operationalization. At another, he tried to revolutionize the existing political milieu by introducing morality in the public realm. The personally-valuable was, thus, meaningfully converged with the socially and the politically-valuable. As the specific features of morality are engendered by the social and historical compulsions of the times, Gandhian conceptualization of political morality is primarily explainable with reference to specific historicity, although transhistorical significance of his ideas is equally relevant.

To reclaim the present, Gandhi thought it necessary to reclaim the past, not in a wholesale manner, but as selective adaptation of its meaningful heritage. He saw immense possibilities of regeneration and innovation in going back to the roots. It was also a mode of engagement with culture. Engagement with culture is often taken as a stance of conservatism but Gandhi's engagement with culture, through symbolism, is a unique stance of innovative praxis and radical vision. It is important to note that Gandhi is neither a complete traditionalist nor an ostensible modernist nor even a post-modernist, in a technical sense, though he shares important ground with all of them. Gandhi, to use Habib's expression, is a 'classical modern figure', in our view.[8]

Gandhian symbolism is a conscious confrontation with and an effective challenge to all forms of hegemony—whether indigenous elitism or alien imperialism. Taking it as a point of strength, rather than inhibition, Gandhi imaginatively used symbolism as a 'unitive' vision, comparable to Goethe's conception of the 'secular in the sacred'. In Gandhi's view, as discussed in the previous chapters, Indian culture and tradition, rich in philosophical nuance and religio-spiritual subtlety, was a valuable resource for cosmopolitan ethical/political vision. Going back to the roots and reminding people of their powerful heritage was a sagacious political move, in the given colonial situation. Aware of the perils of obscurantism usually accompanying appeal to the past, Gandhi undertook the task of constantly reinterpreting, in modern terms, the traditional myths, icons, images, scriptures and adapting them for the renovative, reformist and revolutionary objectives. It is in terms of a 'radical ethic' that Gandhi makes use of the past and succeeds in turning it into a basis of radical politics. And, this makes his endeavour distinctive, in both historico-political and theoretical terms.

Gandhi was astute enough to realize that it is not for the abstract metaphysical components but for a comprehensible content of truth (as ideal and as reality) that symbols are valuable in politics. He selected the right symbols, as indeed he himself created new powerful symbols, and through an insightful deciphering and convincing communication of the entire range of associations invoked by the selected symbols, he could construct a broad spectrum of what might be called a 'shared political reality' in both cognitive/perceptive and practical/actual terms. The political reality of a social entity inheres in people's perception of that reality as much as on its actuality. Gandhi was too much of a realist to have missed this fact.

Gandhi was equally aware that as symbols lose their significance and appeal with changes in the context, they should be renewed, reinterpreted and adapted in consonance with the changing situations. Gandhian symbolism though rooted in the cultural tradition of India, is not narrowly 'contextual', 'located' and 'dated'. It transcends its context, locale and historicity in its universalist, humanist concerns. Disapproving of the reason-emotion, subject-object and private-public dichotomies, Gandhian symbolism also brings into focus the intersubjective dimensions of collective behaviour. This gives his political praxis a specific authenticity and his theorization an innovative insight.

Gandhi was not unaware that symbols are double-edged. They can drive people forward or interrupt their motion, draw people together or hold them apart. Hence the Herculean task of ensuring meaningful political praxis, for a symbolist leader—the task ably carried out by Gandhi, and to an amazing extent, in times with little facilities of mass communication, and abysmally low levels of education and awareness. The subjectivity of the recipients was a challenging scenario. The symbolist strategy was Gandhi's mode of coming to terms with this scenario.

Gandhi's symbolist leadership operated at multiple levels. People identified with him. They were moved by his image of simplicity, sincerity and genuineness. They responded to him without reservations. He worked on the masses, sometimes prior to, at others, without or even in spite of, organizational efforts. People were often unable to describe precisely what

Gandhi delivered to them. Probably, they were made to discover for themselves, what they wanted or what they ought to want, or trust and accept, what he had discovered for them. He was the "man of the people" in a true sense, who took them along to raise the fundamental questions of honourable existence and dignified life in a colonial context. He reverberated both the minds and the conscience of the people, in his times. People gave him unqualified trust. He became the supreme symbol of resurgent India. He symbolized the nation in its true essence.

Gandhian symbolism, in substance, is a civilizational argument. First and foremost, Gandhi remains the pioneer thinker-activist to have challenged the arrogant imperialist west-centric worldview on both theoretical and practical planes and to have articulated an alternative worldview.

Gandhi's simultaneous foray into the past and reconsideration of 'the present' compelled him to search for an alternative order. To address the Gandhian alternative is, thus, also to confront the challenging ethos of our times, in relation to both our heritage and the future vision. Gandhi's ideal order, as discussed in the previous chapters, is premised on his conception of good life, ethic of austerity, nonviolence, communitarian bonds and appropriate technology. It is a non-authoritarian liberatory-communitarian order. Gandhi, on the one hand, insists on bringing back the individual to the centre of the politico-economic order and, on the other, on treating the self (and its autonomy) and the community as mutually constitutive. In an important sense, Gandhian symbolism acquires a cosmopolitan dimension through a generalization of small group norms on the basis of personal conscience.

The key question in any discussion of an ideal is whether and to what extent can human existence be given ideal—moral meaning. It is often questioned whether people's material needs can be satisfied in a way that would preclude exploitation, whether society can rest on trust or politics on transparency. Gandhi's answer is an emphatic affirmative. Gandhi himself describes an ideal as "Euclid's straight line". It is understandable if we accept an ideal as a general dynamic concept which is eventually formed on the basis of an interpretation of existing reality, though it does not correspond to its existing state and which is a constant reminder of the tasks ahead to transform the prevailing reality, in quest of an aspired future. Gandhi's alternative of a humane, decentralized nonviolent politico-economic order and a non-hegemonic global order—far from being regressive, as is often alleged in view of his appeal to the past—is, in our view, a timely corrective to the misplaced priorities of the contemporary development-modernization model. Gandhi's alternative is a plea for reinstating the 'humane', that has been displaced by the modern industrial/commercial/technicist view of life and socio-political order.

The Gandhian worldview, in most clear terms, is a rejection of the expansive state, gigantic economy, repressive technology, oppressive social structure, homogenizing culture and hegemonizing politics. It is a revolt against all structures of domination, as manifestations of violence and violations of human integrity and dignity. His *sarvodaya* ideal, *swaraj* in an ultimate sense, is an emancipatory egalitarian-communitarian utopia—visualizing liberation of all—till the last man in the que. In a very specific sense, it is an advocacy, for the 'small' for its connectivity, interactivity and intersubjectivity. The 'small' in the Gandhian discourse is ethical as well as radical, it is in essence 'humane', the microcosm of the humanity, so as to say. To be "one's own self" is genuine *swaraj* for Gandhi. Gandhian philosophy, is a timely reminder—to regain 'selfhood'—to the present-day humanity, getting increasingly distanced from its own self, whether in terms of the spiralling globalizing, hegemonizing ambitions or in terms of its victimization. To be "one's own self" is to be sure of one's identity and essence, autonomy and freedom. It is a bold and militant acknowledgement of one's individuality though reciprocally rooted in the community, in Gandhi's view. Today, probably as never before, the radical stance of Gandhi needs to be articulated, once again, in terms of radical praxis, as Gandhi himself did in his own times.

Heraclitus talked about the impossibility of specifying the limits of mind. Gandhi was convinced of the infiniteness of the moral potential of the humans and their capabilities for redemption of the self as of the humanity. His praxis vindicated his vision. The Gandhian paradigm, therefore, to recall the idiom of philosopher, Paul Ricoeur is valuable not only in terms of *signification* (contextualized and situation specific) but also of *symbolization* (transcending the situation-specific). Perhaps, therein lies its true salience.

Notes

1. *Young India*, June 1, 1921, p.170.
2. It is pertinent to recall and remember a very significant statement from Gandhi: "... a civilization or a condition in which all the forces fly away from the centre must necessarily be without a goal, whereas those which converge to a point have always a goal. It is then necessary for these two civilizations to meet and we shall have a different force altogether by no means, a menacing force, by no means a force that disunites, but a force that unites. The two forces are undoubtedly opposing forces, but perhaps in the economy of nature both are necessary. Only we, as intelligent human beings with heart and soul, have to see what those forces are, and have to use them, not blindly but intelligently, not

anyhow and haphazard, but with a goal in view. Immediately that is done, there is no difficulty whatsoever in the two civilizations meeting and meeting for a good purpose.

SW, Vol. VI, p. 280.

3. See for an interesting comparison, Bauman's assessment of "Occidental rationality". Z. Bauman, *Legislators and Interpreters: on Modernity, Postmodernity and Intellectuals*, Cambridge, Polity Press, 1987, p. 111.
4. See Jurgen Habermas, *The Philosophical Discourse of Modernity*, Cambridge, Polity Press, 1987.
5. Gandhi's discrimination is important: "There is nothing to prevent me from profiting by the light that may come from the West, only... I must not mistake the glamour for true light", *Harijan*, January 13, 1940, p. 414.
6. D. Noble, "Present Tense Technology", *Democracy*, Vol. 3, Nos. 2-4, 1983, p. 20.
7. Calinescu's desynonymisation of 'modern' and 'contemporary' is significant in this context. See M. Calinescu, *Faces of Modernity*, London, Indiana University Press, 1977, p. 86.
8. See Irfan Habib, "Gandhi and the National Movement", *Social Scientist*, Vol. 23, Nos. 4-6, April-June 1995, p. 8.
9. Gandhi's optimism is notable: "Men often hesitate to make a beginning, because they feel that the objective cannot be achieved in its entirety. This attitude of mind is our greatest obstacle to progress—an obstacle that each man, if he only wills it, can clear away".

   SW, Vol. VI, p. 260.

Bibliography

Allport, Floyed H. *Theories of Perception and Concept of Structure*, New York, Wiley, 1957.

Andreyeva, G. *Social Psychology*, Moscow, Progress, 1980.

Arendt, Hannah. *Men in Dark Times*, New York, Harcourt, Brace and World, 1968.

Ashe, Geoffrey. *Gandhi: A Study in Revolution*, Calcutta, Asia, 1968.

Bandopadhyaya, J. *Social and Political Thought of Gandhi*, Bombay, Allied, 1969.

Bauman, Z. *Legislators and Interpreters: On Modernity, Postmodernity and Intellectuals*, Cambridge, Polity Press, 1987.

Blanshard, Brand. *The Nature of Thought*, Vol. I, New York, Macmillan, 1940.

Bondurant, Joan V. *Conquest of Violence: The Gandhian Philosophy of Conflict* (Rev. ed.) Berkeley, University of California Press, 1967.

Bose, N.K. (ed.), *Selections From Gandhi*, Ahmedabad, Navajivan, 1948.

---, *Studies in Gandhism*, Ahmedabad, Navajivan, 1962.

Brown, Judith M. *Gandhi and Civil Disobedience: The Mahatma in Indian Politics*-1928-34, CUP, 1977.

Browner, S.C. and Kellner, D.M. *Critical Theory And Society: A Reader*, New York, Routledge, 1989.

Bryson, L. *et. al*, *Symbols and Values: An Initial Study*, New York, Harper & Brothers, 1954.

Carnap, Rudolf. *Logical Foundations of Probability*, Chicago, University of Chicago Press, 1950.

Cassirer, Ernst. *The Philosophy of Symbolic Forms* (1923) 3 Vols. (Trans. R. Manheim) New Haven, Yale University Press, 1953-57.

Cobb, Roger W. "The Belief Systems Perspective," *Journal of Politics*, 35, 1 February 1973, 121-153.

Dahl, Robert. *Democracy and Its Critics*, Delhi, Orient Longman, 1991.

Derrida, Jacques. *Writing and Difference* (trans. Alan Blass), Chicago, University of Chicago Press, 1978.

Desai, Mahadev. (ed.) *The Gospel of Selfless Action or the Gita According to Gandhi*, Ahmedabad, Navajivan, 1956.

— *The Diary of Mahadev Desai*, I (trans. & ed. V.G. Desai), Ahmedabad, Navajivan, 1953.

Dewey, John. *Logic: The Theory of Inquiry*, New York, Henry Holt & Co., 1938

Dhawan, G.N. *The Political Philosophy of Mahatma Gandhi*, New Delhi, Gandhi Peace Foundation, 1990.

Douglas, Mary. *Natural Symbols*, London, Cresset, 1970.

Eliade, Mircea. *Images and Symbols* (trans, P. Mairet), New York, Sheed & Ward, 1969.

— *Patterns in Comparative Religion*, Princeton, Bollingen Series, 1970.

Erikson, Eric H. *Life History and the Historical Moment*, New York, W.W. Norton & Co., 1975.

— *Gandhi's Truth*, New York, W.W. Norton & Co., 1969.

Featherstone, *M. Consumer Culture and Postmodernism*, London, Sage, 1991.

Festinger, Leon. *A Theory of Cognitive Dissonance*, Evanston, I11, Row-Peterson, 1957.

Feyerabend, Paul K. *Against Method: Outline of an Anarchistic Theory of Knowledge*, London, New Left Books, 1975.

Firth, Raymond. *Symbols: Public and Private*, Ithaca, Cornell University Press, 1973.

Foucault, M. *The Order of Things*, New York, Random House, 1970.

Gandhi, M.K. *An Autobiography*, Ahmedabad, Navajivan, 1966.

— *Constructive Programme: Its Meaning and Place*, Ahmedabad, Navajivan, 1945.

— *Correspondence with the Government: 1944-47*, Ahmedabad, Navajivan, 1959.

— *Democracy: Real and Deceptive* (comp. R.K. Prabhu) Ahmedabad, Navajivan, 1961.

— *Ethical Religion*, Madras, Ganesan, 1922.

— *From Yarvada Mandir* (trans. V.G. Desai), Ahmedabad, Navajivan, 1957.

— *Hind Swaraj* (1909), Ahmedabad, Navajivan, 1938.

— *The Ideology of the Charkha*, (comp. S. Jaju) Varanasi, Sarva Seva Sangh, 1951.

— *Khadi: Why and How*, Ahmedabad, Navajivan, (1955) 1959.

— *My Religion* (ed. Bharatan Kumarappa), Ahmedabad, Navajivan, (1955)-1985.

— *Non-violence in Peace and War*, Vol. I (1942), Ahmedabad, Navajivan, 1962.

— *Satyagraha in South Africa* (1928), Ahmedabad, Navajivan 1993.

— *Speeches and Writings of Mahatma Gandhi*, Madras, Natesan and Co., 1933.

— *The Collected Works of Mahatma Gandhi*, Delhi, The Publications Division, Ministry of Information and Broadcasting, Government of India, 1959.

— *The Selected Works of Mahatma Gandhi*, (ed., Shriman Narayan), Ahmedabad, Navajivan, 1968.

— *Swaraj Through Charkha*, (Comp. Kanu Gandhi) Sevagram, All India Spinners Association, 1945.

— *Truth is God*, Ahmedabad, Navajivan, 1959.

Geertz, Clifford. *The Interpretation of Cultures*, New York, Basic Books, 1973.

Goffman, Erving. *Behaviour in Public Places*, New York, Free Press, 1963.

Gosavi, D.K. *Tilak, Gandhi and Gita*, Bombay, Bhartiya Vidya Bhavan, 1983.

Gramsci, Antonio. *Selections from the Prison Note Books*, (O. Hoare and G.N. Smith ed. & trans.), London, Lawrence and Wishart, 1971.

Gregg, R.B. *The Power of Non-Violence*, Ahmedabad, Navajivan, 1960.

Gregg, Richard B. *Symbolic Inducement and Knowing: A Study in the Foundations of Rhetoric*, Columbia, University of South Carolina Press, 1984.

Habermas, Jurgen. *The Philosophical Discourse of Modernity*, Cambridge, Polity Press, 1987.

Habib, Irfan. "Gandhi and the National Movement," *Social Scientist*, 23, 4-6, April-June 1995, pp. 3-15.

Hall, Edward T. *The Silent Language*, New York, Doubleday, 1959.

Held, David. (ed.), *Political Theory Today*, California, Stanford University Press, 1991.

Horkheimer, M. *Eclipse of Reason*, New York, Seabury, 1947.

Iyer, Raghavan. *The Moral and Political Thought of Mahatma Gandhi*, Delhi, Oxford University Press, 1973.

---- (ed.) *The Moral and Political Writings of Mahatma Gandhi*, 3 Vols., Oxford, Clarendon, 1985, 1986, 1987.

Jacobson, Norman. "Political Science and Political Education," *American Political Science Review*, 57, 3, Sept. 1963, pp. 561-569.

Jinnah: Speeches as Governor General of Pakistan: 1947-48, Karachi, Government of Pakistan Publication, n.d.

Jung, Carl G. *Psyche and Symbol* (ed. Violet S.de Laszlo), New York, Doubleday, 1958.

Kaushik, Asha. "Creation of Pakistan: Ideological Ambivalence of Theo-Politics," *South Asian Studies*, 31, 1 & 2, Jan-Dec 1996, pp. 100-112.

---- (ed.), *Democratic Concerns: The Indian Experience*, 2 Vols., Jaipur, Aalekh, 1994.

---- and Kaushik, S.N. "Religion as Political Ideology: The Separatist Crusade of Jinnah," *South Asian Studies*, 29-2, July-Dec., 1994, pp. 1-10

---- "The Inverted Pyramid and Gandhi's Counter-directional Paradigm," *Political Science Review*, Vol.32, 1-4, Jan-Dec, 1993, pp. 66-74.

— *Politics, Aesthetics and Culture*, New Delhi, Manohar, 1988.

Kertzer, David I. *Ritual, Politics and Power*, New Haven, Yale University Press, 1988.

Kessler, S. *Islam and Politics in a Malay State*, Ithaca, Cornell University Press, 1978.

Kishwar, Madhu. 'Gandhi on Women', *Economic and Political Weekly*, Oct. 5, 1985, pp. 1691-1702.

Klapp, Orrin E. *Symbolic Leaders: Public Dramas and Public Men*, Aldine, Chicago, 1964.

Kripalani, J.B. *Gandhi: The Statesman*, Delhi, Ranjit Publishers, 1951.

Krishnamurti, Y.G. *Gandhism for Millions*, Patna, Pustak Bhandar, 1949.

Laitin, David. *Hegemony and Culture*, Chicago, Chicago University Press, 1986.

Langer, Susanne K. *Feeling and Form: A Theory of Art*, New York, Scribner, 1953.

— *Philosophy in a New Key*, New York, New American Library, 1942.

Lasswell, Harold D. and Kaplan, Abraham. *Power and Society: A Framework for Political Inquiry*, New Haven, Yale University Press, 1950.

Leach, Edmund. *Culture and Communication*, Cambridge, Cambridge University Press, 1972.

Leiss, William. *The Domination of Nature*, New York, George Braziller, 1972.

Leontiev, A.N. *Problems of the Development of Mind*, Moscow, Progress, 1972.

MacIntyre, Alasdair. *After Virtue*, Notre Dame, University of Notre Dame Press, 1981.

Marcuse, Herbert. *One Dimensional Man: Studies in the Ideology of Advanced Industrial Society*, Boston, Beacon, 1964.

Marx, Karl. *Critique of Hegel's "Philosophy of Right"* (A John and J.O. Malley *Trans*), Cambridge, Cambridge University Press, 1970.

— *Economic and Philosophic Manuscripts of 1844*, Moscow, Progress, 1974.

Mehta, V.R. *Ideology, Modernization and Politics in India*, Delhi, Manohar, 1983.

Morris, Charles. *Signs, Language and Behaviour*, Chicago, Chicago University Press, 1945.

Mukerjee, Radhakamal. *The Way of Humanism: East and West*, New Delhi, Academic Books, 1968.

Mukherjee, Hiren. *Gandhiji: A Study*, New Delhi, People's Publishing House, 1979.

Murti, V.V. Ramana. "Buber's Dialogue and Gandhi's Satyagraha", *The Journal of the History of Ideas*, 29, 1968, pp. 605-613.

Namboodiripad, E.M.S. *The Mahatma and the Ism*, Bombay, People's Publishing House, 1959.

Nanda, B.R. *Gandhi and His Critics*, Delhi, Oxford Paperbacks, 1993.

— *Mahatma Gandhi* (1958) Delhi, Oxford India Paperbacks, 1989.

Nandy, Ashis. *At the Edge of Psychology: Essays in Politics and Culture*, Delhi, Oxford University, Press, 1980.

Narayan, J.P. *From Socialism to Sarvodaya*, Madras, Socialist Book Centre, 1956.

— *Swaraj for the People*, Varanasi, Sarva Seva Sangh, 1977.

Nehru, Jawaharlal. *An Autobiography*, Bombay, Allied, 1962.

— *The Discovery of India*, (1946) New Delhi, Oxford University Press 1981.

Nelson, John S. (ed) *What Should Political Theory Be Now?* Albany, State University of New York Press, 1983.

Novak, Michael. *Choosing Our King: Powerful Symbols in Presidential Politics*, New York, MacMillan, 1974.

Oakeshott, Michael. *Rationalism in Politics*, New York, Basic Books, 1962.

Paige, Glenn D. "Gandhi's Contribution to Global Non-Violent Awakening", *Gandhi Marg*, 12,4, Jan-March, 1991, pp. 429-443.

Panov, V.G. *Emotions, Myths and Theories*, Moscow, Progress, 1985.

Pantham, Thomas. "Thinking with Mahatma Gandhi: Beyond Liberal Democracy," *Political Theory*, II, 2, 1983, pp. 165-168.

Patel, Sujata. "Construction and Reconstruction of Woman in Gandhi", *Economic and Political Weekly*, Feb. 20, 1988, pp 377-387.

Peirce, Charles S. *Values in a Universe of Chance, Selected Writings*, (ed., P.P. Weiner) New York, Doubleday 1958.

Polak, H.S. Brailsford, H.N. and Lawrence, Lord Pethick. *Mahatma Gandhi*, London, Odhams Press, 1949.

Prasad, Rajendra. *At the Feet of Mahatma Gandhi*, Calcutta, Asia, 1961.

Pyarelal. *Towards New Horizons*, Ahmedabad, Navajivan, 1959.

Radhakrishnan, S. *The Bhagwad Gita*, London, George Allen & Unwin, 1970.

--- *An Idealist View of Life*, London, Unwin Books, 1961.

Rajan, R. Sundara. *Towards a Critique of Cultural Reason*, Delhi, Oxford University Press, 1987.

Rajgopalachari, C. *Gandhiji's Teachings and Philosophy*, Bombay, Bhartiya Vidya Bhavan, 1963.

Rao, V.K.R.V. *The Gandhian Alternative to Western Socialism*, Bombay, Bhartiya Vidya Bhavan, 1970.

Rorty, A.O. (ed.) *Explaining Emotions*, Berkeley, University of California Press, 1980.

Roy, Ramashray. *Self and Society: A Study in Gandhian Thought*, New Delhi, Sage, 1984.

--- *Understanding Gandhi*, Delhi, Ajanta, 1996.

Rudolph, S.H. and Rudolph, L.I. *Gandhi: The Traditional Roots of Charisma*, Hyderabad, Orient Longman, 1987.

Ruesch, Jurgen and Kees, Weldon. *Non-Verbal Communication*, Berkeley, University of California Press, 1956.

Russell, Bertrand. *Human Knowledge: Its Scope and Limits*, New York, Simon & Schuster, 1948.

Shridharani, K. *War Without Violence*, Bombay, Bhartiya Vidya Bhavan, 1962.

Shukla, Chandra Shankar. *Conversations of Gandhiji*, Bombay, Vora & Co., 1949.

— *Gandhi's View of Life*, Bombay, Bhartiya Vidya Bhavan, 1951.

Tilak, Bal Gangadhar. *Gita Rahasya or The Science of Karmyoga*, (2 volumes), Poona, Tilak Brothers, 1936.

Turner, Victor. *Dramas, Fields and Metaphors*, Ithaca, Cornell University Press, 1974.

Ulyanovsky, R. *Three Leaders*, Moscow, Progress, 1986.

Walzer, Michael. "Philosophy and Democracy," *Political Theory*, 9, 3, August 1981, pp. 379-399.

Weber, Thomas. *Conflict Resolution and Gandhian Ethics*, New Delhi, The Gandhi Peace Foundation, 1991.

White, Leslie A. *The Science of Culture*, New York, Farrar, Strauss and Cudahy 1959.

Wilden, A. *System and Structure*, London, Tavistock, 1972.

Williams, Raymond. *Marxism and Literature*, Oxford, Oxford University Press, 1977.

Wolpert, Stanley. *Jinnah of Pakistan*, Delhi, Oxford University Press, 1985.

Wright, Philip Wheel. *Metaphor and Reality*, Bloomington, Indiana University Press, 1962.

Index